EXPLORING CUMBRIAN HISTORY

EXPLORING
CUMBRIAN
HISTORY

PHILIP NIXON

breedon **books**
PUBLISHING

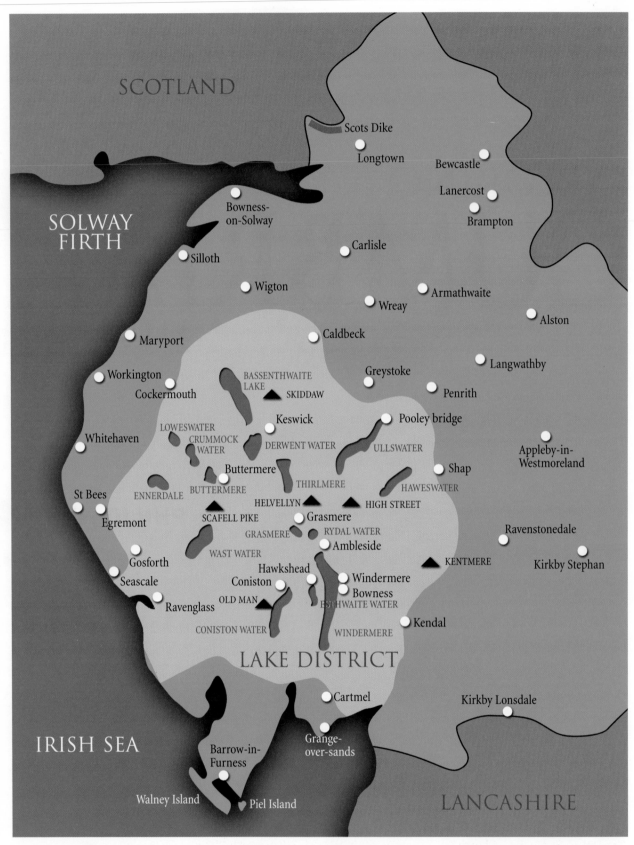

First published in Great Britain in 2009 by The Breedon Books Publishing Company Limited, Breedon House, 3 The Parker Centre, Derby, DE21 4SZ.

© Philip Nixon, 2009

ISBN 978-1-85983-728-3
Printed and bound by Gutenberg Press Ltd, Malta.

CONTENTS

AUTHOR'S NOTE

I have included an author's note in this book, in spite of the uncanny feeling that no one reads them.

This book has been produced to be entertaining while still providing enough information to satisfy the curious – but, hopefully, it will also encourage a deeper and more intense exploration of the history of Cumbria. I have also chosen subjects that I hope are visually stimulating in their own way and these too may encourage further exploration with the camera.

With a vast subject like the history of Cumbria it is not so much what is included that is important as what is included out – so to speak. However, this project really has been most enjoyable: both the photography and the research have been endlessly interesting. I have always had a terrific affinity and fascination with the counties of Cumberland and Westmorland and, it necessarily follows, their progeny of Cumbria.

When I was very young my Great-Uncle Jim married my Auntie Gladys – he was from Durham and she was from Cumberland. What a wonderful lady – I could see why he married her. She was a little woman with a wonderful fresh complexion, sparkling eyes and a ready smile, and her accent was just marvellous. She made everyone most welcome in the relaxed, warm and friendly atmosphere of their family home, and I decided, even at that young age, that Cumberland must be a wonderful place and that I would love to go there.

Coincidentally, my brother-in-law also married a 'bonny Cumbrian lass', and she and her family are great ambassadors for the county with their friendly warmth, sense of humour and great generosity.

While writing and photographing *Exploring Cumbrian History* I have enjoyed the support and help of many of my family and friends, together with a great deal of help from the people who lived in the places I visited, and I would like to convey my most sincere thanks to them all.

ACKNOWLEDGEMENTS

Grateful thanks to the following for their invaluable help and encouragement with this book:

To my family – Valerie Nixon, Mark Nixon, Sophy Nixon, Adrian Briggs and Archie the Labrador; to my friends John Stephenson and John Humphries, for their help and their valuable and entertaining company; to my past co-authors, Denis Dunlop and Hugh Dias; and also to the following: Tullie House Museum, Carlisle Cathedral, Carlisle Castle and Hawkshead Old Grammar School; and, of course, to Michelle and the rest of the excellent and professional team at Breedon Books.

Finally, to past Cumbrians Uncle Jim and Auntie Gladys, and present Cumbrians David, Shiela, Richard and Kerryl.

INTRODUCTION

Cumbria is the second-largest county in England. When one thinks of Cumbria it is usually the Lake District National Park that springs to mind, but Cumbria is much more: for example it was here that the British Celts fought to preserve their independence from the Saxons, and the Norse influence can still be traced through the place names.

The main centres of population are Carlisle, Penrith, Kendal and the ports of Barrow-in-Furness, Whitehaven and Workington, and the county has a combined population of around half a million lively inhabitants. Carlisle is the county's largest town and the administrative centre. It lies in the north of the county, close to the Scottish border, and for centuries was a base from which the English could launch attacks into Scotland. Carlisle was of great importance during the border conflicts, and at the height of reiving times the city served as the headquarters of the Warden of the West English March and protected England during a constant wave of border raids.

The coast of the county extends along the edge of the Irish Sea from Morecambe Bay to the Solway Firth. There is a large naval shipyard in Barrow-in-Furness and light industry in Workington and Whitehaven, while Britain's chief nuclear fuel reprocessing and recycling centre is also on the coast at Sellafield. Of the county's coastline, the Furness Peninsula is possibly the most beautiful – a place of small but attractive seaside resorts and, indeed, once an area of great ecclesiastical power.

Prehistoric remains have also left their legacy in the many ancient stone circles and burial sites, and the system of Roman forts, roads and other remains found throughout the county serve as a reminder of their long occupation.

Cumbria is famous for its lakes and mountains, and the Lake District National Park not only has England's largest lake, Windermere, but also the country's highest mountain, Scafell Pike. It is an area of magnificent crags, expansive fells and huge lakes, and it is no wonder that this dramatic landscape inspired Wordsworth and many other poets and artists. There are also historic houses set in beautiful gardens, ancient stone circles, abbeys and churches reflecting past glories and museums that tell the story of Cumbria.

Notable inhabitants like Beatrix Potter, William Wordsworth, Lady Anne Clifford, John Ruskin and Sara Losh have all made a contribution to the history of the county.

As well as the more well-known sites in the county such as Carlisle Castle and the cathedral, it also has a wealth of hidden gems, like Hawkshead Old Grammar School, with its knowledgeable, enthusiastic and helpful curator; Wreay Church, a masterpiece by a talented female architect; and, of course, the hidden back streets of the wonderful market town of Kendal. They all combine to provide much enjoyable material for the endlessly fascinating exploration of this wonderful county of just over 2,600 square miles.

Opposite: The market cross donated by a former townsman, the Right Hon Sir William Stephenson, who was created Lord Mayor of London in 1764.

Alston is well known for its steep cobbled streets and 17th-century stone buildings.

Alston

Alston is said to be to be the highest market town in England and stands at an altitude of just over 1,000ft above sea level. It is about 20 miles from the nearest town and is approached from every direction across the remote landscape of wild, heather-covered fells that make up the North Pennines Area of Outstanding Natural Beauty. It clings to the upper reaches of the River South Tyne on the very edge of the Eden district of Cumbria. It is well known for its steep cobbled streets, 17th-century stone buildings and its market cross,

which was donated by a former townsman, the Right Hon Sir William Stephenson, who was created Lord Mayor of London in 1764. In addition to the regular markets, sheep and cattle fairs were held in its streets and, even more unusually, wrestling matches and races were regular events in the town.

The route of a Roman road known as the Maiden Way can be traced as it passes the town, a mile or so to the north, on its way to Whitley Castle, an old Roman fort at which the elaborate defensive ditches can still be clearly seen.

There was no mention of Alston in the *Domesday Book* of 1086 because the area was under the control of the Scots at the time. The manor of Alston, which was originally known as Alderstone, is first mentioned in recorded history when it was granted to William de Veteripont by William I 'The Lion', King of Scotland in 1209. By 1280 the area was under the control of the English, but Edward I of England confirmed the ownership as that of the de Veteripont family. Alston then passed by marriage to the Whytlawe family, who, in 1443, granted it to the Stapletons of Edenhall. From them it passed as part of their daughter's dowry to the Hilton family of Durham.

Alston and the surrounding fells have been mined extensively for silver, lead, coal and anthracite since Roman times. In the early 18th century the Quakers had set up the London Lead Mining Company and established a purpose-built mining community (similar to that at Lanark in Scotland) at nearby Nenthead, and by 1718 there were 119 productive mines bringing in an income of about £70,000 a year. Alston grew rapidly in size to accommodate the ever increasing number of workers, though many miners lived at or near their places of work in mineshops, often suffering appalling conditions. Other forms of employment were provided by a brewery, a candle house and a worsted mill.

The unusual 16th-century one-handed clock that once belonged to James Radcliffe, the Earl of Derwentwater.

As mining died out in the mid-1800s, Alston's population decreased. When the demand for lead suffered a heavy decline, unemployed workers had no alternative but to become inmates of the poorhouse. The one in Alston was built around the mid-1700s. Life in the poorhouse was a punishing regime – 10 hours of hard work was done in return for a bed and a meagre diet of porridge, bread and broth with possibly a drop of milk.

Charles Dickens visited Alston in 1838 in the search for background material for his novel, *Nicholas Nickleby*. The town has changed little since then and has provided the location for several costume dramas, films and documentaries.

There has been a church in the town since the mid-12th century; however, the first one fell into ruin and was demolished – a few decorated stones in the church porch are all that remain of this building. A new one was built on the site in 1769; however, it too was demolished when the present St Augustine's was built in 1869. Inside the church is an unusual 16th-century one-handed clock that once belonged to James Radcliffe, the Earl of Derwentwater, whose home was Dilston Hall and whose estate included much of the land around Alston Moor. Radcliffe was the illegitimate grandson of Charles II and a Roman Catholic. He was brought up at the French court along with his royal cousin, James Stuart, son of James II. In 1715 Radcliffe joined the Jacobite Rebellion in Scotland but was captured when the Scots were defeated at Preston. He was condemned for treason and executed on Tower Hill on 24 February 1716, after which his estates were confiscated and his family exiled. Charles Radcliffe, his younger brother, was condemned at the same time but managed to escape to France. However, he was captured at sea while on his way to join Bonnie Prince Charlie and was executed in 1764 – as such he has the dubious distinction of being the last man in England to be publicly beheaded for treason.

In 1735 the Derwentwater Estates were granted to the Greenwich Hospital and in the following years Dilston Hall was demolished. In 1767 the Commissioners of Greenwich Hospital gave the 16th-century clock and a bell to Alston Parish Church – probably for the new church, which was under construction at that time. Although the bell was installed in this new church, and, indeed, in the newer church of 1869, where it is still rung every day, the clock face was lost and never installed. It lay neglected for 200 years until 1977, when the parishioners raised the money to have it repaired and installed.

Today, traditional sheep farming and walkers on the Pennine Way are the main sources of income for the locals. Tourism is also important to the town and the narrow gauge South Tynedale Railway operates trips along the 2¼-mile line in the scenic South Tyne valley between Alston in Cumbria and Kirkhaugh in Northumberland. The line is believed to be the highest in the country and is built along part of the railway trackbed of the former 13-mile-long standard gauge Haltwhistle to Alston branch line, which was closed by British Rail in 1976. Alston Station has a pleasant riverside setting and the train tickets are sold from the restored Victorian station building.

This attractive, traditional market town situated in the heart of the North Pennines is surrounded by a natural beauty that affords unforgettable views in every direction.

Galava – Ambleside Roman Fort

Although these remains do not have the magnificent mountain location of Hardknott Fort or the impressive structure of the Bath *Galava, Ambleside Roman Fort, protected the vital trade routes across Cumbria.*

All forts had granaries or horrea for the storage of grain, which formed the main part of the soldiers' rations.

Waterhead on the northern end of Lake Windermere – the Romans made good use of this strategic position.

one of a line of fortified structures protecting the vital trade routes across Cumbria. The first construction, in the late first century, was probably a small timber fort built to house a small garrison of about 200 men, although this was soon abandoned. However, the site was redeveloped a few years later in the early years of the second century, when the original fort was demolished and a more substantial replacement was built in stone on a man-made raised platform, the outline of which can still be traced. This improved fortification housed a cohort of 500 infantrymen. Between 1914 and 1920 excavations carried out by the eminent archaeologist R.G. Collingwood revealed the remains of the fort's defences and sections of the internal buildings, including the main gate, the south gate, the commanding officer's house or *praetorium*, the headquarters building or *principia*, and the granaries, which today are the most visible remains. All forts were provided with granaries or *horrea* for the efficient storage of grain, which formed the main part of the

House at Ravenglass, Galava is nevertheless set on a beautiful site right beside the spacious open area of Borrans Park at Waterhead on the northern end of Lake Windermere and makes good use of this strategic position, which is well protected by water on two sides. The remains of a road linking the fort with the lakeside suggests that perhaps the Romans used water transport for moving men to and from the south. The first fort was probably built in about AD 79 as

soldiers' rations; although this was supplemented by fruit, vegetables, meat and beer. These long, low, heavily buttressed buildings had raised wooden floors allowing good ventilation that would keep the grain dry, which was most likely stored in large bins or sacks.

Galava is well worth a visit – the site provides much thought and speculation upon what it was like for these soldiers manning the 4ft-thick walls of their small fort in what would have been a wild and dangerous area in those days. Today, the fort is owned by the National Trust but is maintained by English Heritage.

Appleby Horse Fair

In the market town of Appleby-in-Westmorland the horse fair usually takes place during the first week in June – it starts on the first Thursday and ends on the second Wednesday. Its charter was granted by James II and has allowed the legal sale of horses since 1685, and for many centuries sheep and cattle

were also sold at Appleby. It is world-famous and is possibly the largest of its kind, and it attracts a huge gypsy gathering. Romany families travel great distances to meet up with old friends and conduct business. The travellers traditionally camp and establish the fair on a group of fields on a hill on the southern outskirts of Appleby overlooking the town. Originally this was known as Gallows Hill because of its macabre use in earlier times, but over the years it has become known as Fair Hill.

Flashing Lane, the old main road from Appleby to Brampton, is closed to allow sellers to display horses to potential buyers by trotting them back and forth along the roadway. Each

Prospective buyers put the horses through their paces.

The old main road from Appleby to Brampton is closed during the fair to allow sellers to display horses to potential buyers by trotting them back and forth along the roadway.

The best way to give the horses a wash is to get into the river with them.

The traditional washing of the horses in the River Eden always attracts a lot of spectators.

day during the fair horses are led down to the River Eden near the town centre to be washed and groomed ready for the day's trading, and there are no restrictions – anyone can buy. Of course, it is not only horses for sale and for hundreds of years other goods have been sold at the fair. There are over 100 stalls in the field next to Fair Hill selling saddlery, clothing, pottery, books, footwear and various souvenirs,

as well as fortune-tellers, palm-readers and food stalls. It is a quite remarkable experience and during the fair horses can be found almost everywhere – in the river, on its banks, along the roadsides or tethered outside hotels and shops.

Appleby Fair is not formally organised but has gradually developed over the years from an agricultural sale to a major cultural event for

Even though it is a busy time, owners and horses find a little time to relax.

the travelling community. It is, however, overseen in an advisory capacity by a strategic group of district and county councils, Cumbria Constabulary, the RSPCA and other agencies, who diligently ensure the fair's smooth running to provide an enjoyable and memorable event for visitors with the minimum amount of disruption for local residents.

Traditionally, no entrance fee is charged to caravans, horse-sellers or visitors – making it even more enjoyable and memorable.

Appleby-in-Westmorland

Appleby's full name is Appleby-in-Westmorland, and the old county was incorporated into the town's name in 1974 to recognise and preserve it – Appleby was originally the county town of Westmorland. The assize courts were held there, although the county council administered from its offices in Kendal. The town was once a part of Scotland but was transferred to England in 1092; however, it still suffered frequent raids by the Scots and was almost destroyed in 1388. Appleby developed into the market town of Westmorland after the Norman Conquest, probably because of its strategic position in the Eden valley, where it was situated on an easily defendable loop of the River Eden. In 1092 it was King William II who first recognised the town's potential as an economic and administrative centre when he gave Appleby to one of his favourite barons, Ranulph de Meschines. Its first market charter was granted in 1174. It is an attractive market town with a great deal of interest and charm.

The horses and ponies have to look their best.

The cloisters, designed by Sir Robert Smirke in 1811, are situated at the north end of Boroughgate.

Appleby's uncommonly wide main street, Boroughgate, has been described as one of the finest in England. It stretches from the north end, with the remarkable cloisters designed by Sir Robert Smirke in 1811, to the south end, by the impressive castle, which, sadly, is closed to the public. For a while it was the home of the remarkable Lady Anne Clifford, who devoted much of her time and money to restoring the neglected estates, castles and churches in the area. Not far from the entrance to the castle, set in a cobbled courtyard and framed by an archway, now known as the Hospital of St Anne, is a group of almshouses that were established by Lady Anne Clifford in the mid-1650s for 13 poor widows. At that time there were many itinerant beggars, and her concern for old women in dire need inspired her to build this quiet refuge.

During the Civil War the Royalists surrendered Appleby Castle to the Parliamentarians, along with five knights, 25 colonels, nine lieutenant-colonels, six majors, 46 captains, 17 lieutenants, six coronets, three ensigns, five pieces of artillery, 1,200 horses and 1,000 standard arms, not to mention all their baggage and equipment. However, Lady Anne Clifford, Countess of Pembroke, was a confirmed Royalist and after the Civil War she reoccupied the castle and celebrated the return of Charles II to the throne. It was said that she 'thought her gates were then not wide enough to receive her guests, which before had been too wide to receive regiments of Parliamentary soldiers.'

The two town crosses, one at each end of Boroughgate, now mark the places where high

The Hospital of St Anne, a group of almshouses established by Lady Anne Clifford in the mid-1650s for 13 poor widows.

platforms were built for the great festivities hosted by Lady Anne Clifford. The 17th-century High Cross is inscribed *Retain your Loyalty, Preserve your Rights* and the Low Cross is now an 18th-century copy of the original. Appleby was Pitt the Younger's constituency when he became Prime Minister in 1783.

In the middle of the north end of Boroughgate is the 1596 black-and-white Moot Hall. The centuries-old tradition of holding town council meetings on the first floor is still upheld. The ground floor was once occupied by butchers' shops, but it now houses the excellent and friendly tourist information centre. Between here and the cloisters a bull ring can be seen set into the paving – bulls were tethered here for baiting up until 1832. One end of a strong rope was looped around a bull's neck and the other passed through the ring. Several men would pull the bull into position, where it would be held by putting a *twitch* or a simple loop in the rope so it could not move too far – and then the baiting would start.

The old bull ring can still be seen in the market place.

St Lawrence's Church has what is believed to be the oldest working organ in Britain.

The High Cross at the south end of Boroughgate.

Just through the Gothic arcade on the edge of the market square is the 12th-century Church of St Lawrence. The oldest part of the church is the lower part of the tower, which was probably part of an earlier pele tower. The early 14th-century porch with dog-tooth moulding around the entrance is also very striking and worth investigation. The church was burned by the Scots in 1174 and suffered a further destructive Scottish raid, led by Robert the Bruce, in 1388. In the 14th century the tower was opened to the nave, when it was felt it was not necessary for the building to be so defendable. In the 17th century, Lady Anne Clifford restored much of what had been wantonly burned. The church is a great mixture of styles: its perpendicular exterior contrasts markedly with the Early English and Gothic Revival interior. The Clifford Chapel houses Lady Anne's altar tomb, together with an alabaster effigy of her mother, Margaret. The church has what is considered to be the oldest working organ in Britain, which dates from the

St Martin's window, Armathwaite Church.

mid-1500s and was given to St Lawrence's by Carlisle Cathedral in 1683.

Appleby is a small town with a population of about 2,500 and is fairly quiet for most of the year, but at the beginning of June every year it attracts people from all over the world to the colourful and exciting Appleby Horse Fair.

Armathwaite – The Church of Christ and St Mary

The small, simple sandstone Church of Christ and St Mary can be found on the edge of the village of Armathwaite in the beautiful Eden valley. It originally served the parish of Hesket-in-the-Forest as a chapel of ease; these were provided for the convenience of those people living at some distance from the parish church but who were subordinate to it. Others,

The William Morris east window, Armathwaite.

The Church of Christ and St Mary, Armathwaite.

however, were built at the roadside, often near river crossings, for the benefit of travellers.

By 1660 the chapel had fallen into a sorry state of disrepair, but it was later rebuilt by Richard Skelton of Armathwaite Castle. John Skelton, the infamous satirical poet, was of the same family and it was he who upset Cardinal Wolsey with his vigorous satire and only avoided his wrath and any repercussions by taking sanctuary in Westminster Cathedral.

In the church there are some fine examples of stained glass, and the east window has two magnificent panels made by William Morris and Co. They show Christ displaying the nail marks in one panel and Mary, the mother of Jesus, in the other.

Another superb window depicts the story of St Martin, a Roman soldier who cut his cloak in half to share it with a beggar whom he encountered in a street outside the city of Amiens, where he was stationed. The following night he had a dream in which Christ was wearing the cloak and telling a host of angels of Martin's charitable act.

The well-kept little country church of Christ and St Mary remains today much as it was when

Banks Turret – a lonely outpost on Hadrian's Wall.

it was restored in the second half of the 1600s and provides a little haven of peace and tranquillity.

Banks East Turret 52a, Hadrian's Wall

Originally, the western 30 miles of Hadrian's Wall was built of turf with stone turrets. This section stretched from Bowness-on-Solway to Milecastle 49 near the River Irthing. However, within 10 years the turf had been replaced with stone and Banks East Turret was incorporated into its fabric. Turrets were, in effect, simple two-storey stone watchtowers and were built to

a standard plan. There were two of these buildings equidistant between the milecastles, designed as temporary accommodation for soldiers patrolling the wall – the upper floor and roof had ladder access and a wall walk was incorporated into the design.

Barrow-in-Furness

It took just 40 years for the large industrial town of Barrow-in-Furness to develop from a tiny 19th-century hamlet to the biggest iron and steel manufacturing centre in the world, complete with a major shipbuilding industry. In 1845 Barrow was still only a small and remote farming village with only a few thousand inhabitants, but in 1846 the railway was built, thereby allowing iron ore from the Furness mines to be transported to the new deep-water port for shipping. Further development and rapid expansion brought continuing prosperity and by 1870 it had the largest iron works in the world, complete with blast furnaces, to support a huge, thriving shipbuilding industry. By 1864

Barrow had a population of over 8,000 and by 1881 this had increased almost sixfold to over 47,000. The new Victorian boom town, with its wide, well-planned, tree-lined streets, was the creation of two men: Henry Schneider, an industrialist, and Sir James Ramsden, a superintendent of the railway who went on to become the first mayor of Barrow. They founded the Barrow Haematite Iron and Steel Company, built the docks and formed the Barrow Shipbuilding Company – which later became Vickers – covering some 184 acres of

The Needle at Rampside was built between 1850 and 1870 and is the only survivor of a series of 13 lighthouses built on the approaches to Rampside and Barrow. It has been listed as an historic structure.

The Herbert Leigh – Barrow's longest-serving lifeboat. It came into service in 1951 and was retired in 1982. During its service it was launched 136 times and her crew saved 71 lives.

Barrow's striking 'Modern Gothic' town hall can be seen from all over the area.

Barrow Island. Their first steamship, the *Aries*, was built in 1870 and many merchant ships, battleships, oil tankers, passenger liners and submarines followed.

The architecturally striking town hall is in the centre of the town, and its clock tower can be seen from almost anywhere in the area. It was built from local red sandstone and was formally opened in 1887 – a fitting symbol of Barrow's Victorian development. It was designed in the Modern Gothic style by the architect, W.H. Lynn. The richly detailed interior has a beautiful oak-panelled council chamber and the Queen's Hall is blessed with remarkable and vibrant stained-glass windows. There are many fine churches and public buildings in Barrow and almost 300 of them are Grade I or Grade II listed.

Walney Island can be reached by crossing the bridge from Barrow Docks. It is a 10-mile-long offshore island and is reputedly the windiest lowland site in Britain. The island has two important nature reserves: the North Nature Reserve, which is home to Britain's rarest amphibian, the Natterjack Toad, and over 130 species of bird, and the South Nature Reserve, which is believed to be the largest nesting ground for Herring Gulls and Lesser Black Backed Gulls in the whole of Europe.

Between Walney Island and Barrow is the tiny Piel Island, on which can be found the overgrown ruins of the castle, the Ship Inn and a few small houses dating from the 1700s. The island can be reached by crossing the mile-long causeway to Roa Island from Rampside. From

Welney Island, Barrow-in-Furness.

The Piel ferry carries passengers to and from Piel from Roa Island.

there a small boat carries passengers to the island during the summer, subject to tides and weather, of course.

King Stephen granted the island to Furness Abbey in 1127 to provide the monks with a safe harbour from the many raids by the Scots. King John allowed a wooden structure to be built on the island in 1212, in which the abbey could store provisions – allowing ships to unload cargo destined for the abbey.

In the early 14th century Edward III granted Furness Abbey a licence to crenellate the tower and a motte and bailey castle was added, with many stones for the castle taken from the beach

Roa Island is reached by a mile-long causeway from Rampside.

The haunting ruins of Piel Castle from Welney Island.

and roughly worked. Piel Castle not only provided safe storage from pirates but also did a roaring trade in smuggling. Naturally, with the Dissolution of the Monasteries the castle fell into disrepair, and isolated instances of smuggling were recorded right up until 1772 when revenue officers finally put a stop to the activity. The island was given to Barrow Corporation in 1918, and the castle came into state guardianship in 1919 and is now in the care of English Heritage.

Beatrix Potter

Beatrix Potter was born on 28 July 1866 to very wealthy parents in South Kensington, London. She would have been quite lonely at home as she was educated by a governess and consequently had very little contact with other people. However, she did keep quite a few animals as pets, which she studied carefully and made detailed drawings of. She began to be drawn into her own world and created her own stories based on animals. Every year her parents took her on a three-month-long summer holiday. Beatrix was 16 when they first stayed near Ambleside in the Lake District, where she and her younger brother Bertie were allowed the freedom of the woods and fields. Beatrix was very interested in natural history and would spend many hours drawing wildlife such as fungi and flowers. Her parents entertained many eminent guests, including Hardwicke Rawnsley, a local vicar, who eventually became one of the three founders of the National Trust. His strong views on the need to preserve the natural beauty of Lakeland had a profound effect on the young Beatrix, who had developed a great love for the natural beauty of the area.

Many times during her early 20s Beatrix's parents tried to find her a suitable husband, but she always turned them down. She did not care for the idea of being tied down to a repetitive domestic life, staying at home and bringing up children. Instead, she placed great value on her independence and so she remained single and stayed in her own home.

When Beatrix was 27 she wrote an illustrated letter about one of her pet rabbits to a little boy called Noel Moore, the son of an ex-governess. She sent the manuscript to six publishers, but it was turned down. She then paid for the story to be published herself and ordered a private print run of 250 copies. These sold out and the book had to be reprinted. However, it was her friend Canon Rawnsley who persuaded publishers Frederick Warne to look at the book again and this time they offered to take it on, although they did not have much hope it would sell; they actually gave the project to their youngest brother, Norman, as a test for his first project at the company. But Norman proved to be a good choice. He took a great interest in the book…and in Beatrix. He was determined it was going to do well and they worked hard together over the fine details of the book. It was Norman who decided that each drawing of Peter Rabbit should be in colour and Beatrix insisted that the book should remain small so that it would be easy for children to hold. The book was published in 1902, when Beatrix was 36.

The relationship between Norman and Beatrix grew and they soon became engaged. However, Beatrix's parents disapproved because they did not want Beatrix to marry a tradesman. They eventually relented, but insisted that Beatrix should live apart from Norman for six months, in the hope that she would change her mind. Sadly, before the wedding could take place, Norman was diagnosed with leukaemia and died. Beatrix was devastated and she wrote a letter to his sister, Millie, saying 'He did not live long, but he fulfilled a useful, happy life. I must try to make a fresh beginning next year.'

After Norman's death, Beatrix moved to the Lakeland, where she was to live for the rest of

Hill Top – Beatrix Potter's first home in the Lake District.

her life. She bought Hill Top farm in Sawrey in 1905. By the she had a steady income from her books; *Peter Rabbit* had sold over 50,000 copies, and for the next eight years she busied herself writing more books and visiting her farm. In 1909 she bought another farm opposite Hill Top called Castle Farm, which became her main

Castle Farm was a bigger, more convenient home for Beatrix after her marriage to William Heelis.

The Tower Bank Arms features in Beatrix Potter's Jemima Puddleduck.

An old photograph of Beatrix in front of Hill Top with a pet rabbit.

Lakeland base. She wrote 23 books and many were based in or around Hill Top. Characters such as Tom Kitten, Samuel Whiskers and Jemima Puddleduck were all created there, and the books contain many pictures based on the house and garden, leading it to become the most visited literary shrine in the Lake District. Beatrix Potter bought a lot of land and property around Sawrey, including the Old Post Office, Castle Cottage and several small farms. In 1913, aged 47, she married William Heelis, her solicitor from Hawkshead, and moved into Castle Cottage, which was bigger and much more convenient than Hill Top.

With her eyesight failing, Beatrix stopped writing her childrens' books and devoted her time to the breeding of sheep and the conservation of Lakeland farms. From the income from her very successful books and later her inheritance, Beatrix was able to buy several more working farms and moved onto the next stage of her life as a farmer, which lasted for 30 years. In 1923 she bought Troutbeck Park Farm and became a renowned expert on breeding prize-winning Herdwick sheep. Beatrix continued to buy property and in 1930 bought

Beatrix Potter made careful and detailed studies of the many animals she kept as pets.

the Monk Coniston Estate – 4,000 acres that stretched from Little Langdale to Coniston – on which stands Tarn Hows, one of Lakeland's most visited beauty spots.

When she died on 22 December 1943, Beatrix Potter left 14 farms and 4,000 acres of land to the National Trust, together with her magnificent flocks of Herdwick sheep. It was one of the biggest legacies ever made. The trust now owns 91 hill farms, many of which have a mainly Herdwick flock but with a total holding of about 25,000 sheep. This was her gift to the nation; her own beloved countryside for all to enjoy. Beatrix achieved the distinction of being the first woman to be elected president of the Herdwick Sheepbreeders' Association, which still continues to do its valuable work.

Bewcastle

In AD 122 the Roman Emperor Hadrian ordered the building of a stone and turf fortification across the width of northern England. A number of outpost forts were built and one of these was built at Bewcastle and had a direct link with the wall at Birdoswald.

It was an important site in the second and third centuries with 1,000 troops – the First Nervan Cohort of Germans – garrisoned here. It is somewhat unclear as to what happened after the Romans left in AD 637 but the fact that a significant Anglo-Saxon cross was erected here indicates that the site must have been of great religious importance.

The earliest recorded church dates from 1277 and the reign of Edward I, though only the east end now remains. Building material was taken directly from the ready-made supply of the Roman fort's remains. The present church was rebuilt in 1792 when its dedication was changed to that of St Cuthbert. The Bewcastle Cross in the churchyard is of particular note and possibly dates from sometime around AD 675 and the time of Benedict Biscop. It is inscribed with runes and enigmatic figures, providing much material for speculation, discussion and research. It is accepted to be,

Beatrix Potter was the first woman to be elected president of the Herdwick Sheepbreeders' Association.

The Bewcastle Cross is thought to be the finest example of an Anglo-Saxon cross in the whole of Europe.

St Cuthbert's Church in Bewcastle is reputed to have had some shady rectors.

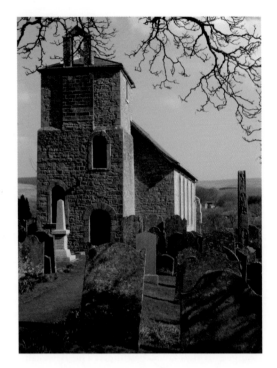

along with the Ruthwell Cross in Scotland, one of the finest examples of an Anglo–Saxon cross in the whole of Europe.

Suggestions have been made, based on the sundial on the cross, that there may have been a monastic cell within the remains of the Roman fort. If the seventh-century cross is in its original position it is quite possible that there was a religious building here at that time.

The shady history of some of the past rectors suggests that they were successful reivers, clearly identifying closely with their flock. The graveyard has many interesting headstones bearing the names of the more notable Border Reivers clans – Armstrong, Elliott, Nixon and Routledge – and the oldest dates from 1698.

It is probably safe to say that at some time nearly every able-bodied man in Bewcastle was involved in reiving. Even the local vicar was drawn in, despite the fact that the church is next door to the castle. His name appears on a list of complaints made by the Scots against the English in 1552. It mentions the Grahams (see Brackenhill Tower) – particularly George of the Gingles – plus Will Patrick, priest of Bewcastle, helped by his curate John Nelson, when they lifted a substantial number of cattle on a raid.

The castle was originally built soon after 1092, using part of the Roman ditch system and probably constructed of timber. The present stone castle was built, using material from the Roman fort, by one of Edward III's generals,

Bewcastle Castle was one of the strongholds of the Warden of the West March and was built in an attempt to curtail incursions by Scottish reivers.

John de Strivelyn, between 1340 and 1360. Falling into disrepair under the de Middleton family, it was thought to have been repaired by the Warden of the English West March, the Duke of Gloucester, who later became Richard III. From the late 15th century until 1608 it was held for the Crown by the Musgraves, who acted as constables.

Official positions in the area were variously filled by the Salkelds, the Lowthers, the Carletons, the Musgraves and the Dacres; although sometimes it was difficult to tell whose side they were on. A wry comment by Thomas Musgrave sums up the situation, 'They are a people that will be Scottish when they will and English at their pleasure'. However, when Musgrave lost the constable's position at Bewcastle to William, Lord Dacre, it is said that he stole all the lead and broke all the windows in a fit of anger – fuelled, no doubt, by the fact that the Mugraves and the Dacres had been feuding for the best part of 300 years.

In the late 15th century a large-scale attack, mounted by the Armstrongs and their associates and led by Lord Maxwell, Warden of the Scottish West March, saw extensive damage inflicted on the castle, the surrounding buildings and the barmkin (a Scottish term for a defensive enclosure, often found at small castles or pele towers).

Reivers made good use of the green track leading through the Bewcastle Wastes – this had been the Roman Maiden Way – as their road from Birdoswald.

Birdoswald Roman Fort

Birdoswald enjoys what is perhaps one of the most picturesque settings along the whole of Hadrian's Wall, overlooking the gorge of the River Irthing. It is interesting because at no other point along the wall can all the components of the Roman frontier system be found in such a small area. The fort at Birdoswald was constructed on a rocky spur, a perfect position that would have afforded extra protection to its southern flanks. However, so that they could make use of this natural feature, the Romans had to use great effort and

The east gate at Birdoswald Roman Fort.

Birdoswald Roman Fort occupies one of the most picturesque situations on Hadrian's Wall.

ingenuity to drain the land and then construct their fort of turf and timber. The northern perimeter wall of Birdoswald would have been incorporated into Hadrian's Wall, which was also built from turf at that time. The *vallum*, or defensive ditch, can still be seen to the south of the later stone curtain wall and was almost certainly intended to be used as part of the defences of the early fort.

Sometime in the early second century the decision was taken to rebuild Birdoswald Roman Fort in stone. It was also extended, thereby making the north wall of the fort extend beyond Hadrian's Wall and creating the need for an east and west gate adjoining the wall. Most forts of this type had four main arched entrances set roughly in the centre of each of the four perimeter walls, but at Birdoswald the east and west entrances were off-centre, leaving a large area of perimeter wall to the south with only a single gate. Because of this two further gates were added on the east and west walls, giving more ready access to the southern military zone.

Birdoswald Fort itself is of a traditional standard Roman design and is in the shape of a playing card: that is, rectangular with rounded corners for greater strength. Originally the walls would have been about 14ft (4.2m) high to a wall walk, and on top of that there would have been a crenellated parapet another 6ft (1.8m) high to afford protection for the soldiers on guard. The fort had defensive towers on the four corners, and two of the bases can still be seen at the north-west and south-east corners. Each of the gates would also have had defensive towers, the main double gates would have had a tower at each side of the opening and the two additional single gates would have each had a tower above.

Some of the internal buildings were also constructed at this time, four of which were to the north of the original wall line. Two of these were long, rectangular buildings and were probably used for storage. The foundations of one can be seen in front of the existing farmhouse, but the other one has been reburied and lies further to the east. However, the most remarkable find at Birdoswald was a *basilica*, a large aisled hall used for drill practice and exercise, located in the north-west quarter of the fort. It is thought to be unique because no building of this type has ever been found inside a Roman fort.

In 1929 a barrack block was excavated just beyond the eastern store building in the north-east quarter, but this has also been reburied. The contours of the headquarters building can still be made out near the east gate, and again it probably also dates from the time of Emperor Hadrian, but it has not been fully excavated and so the details are not certain. Around the time of Hadrian's death, about AD 138, it was decided to rebuild the existing turf wall in stone. The line of the new stone wall was moved further north and so joined Birdoswald at its northern corners, in a somewhat similar style to the original turf and timber fort. Because of this change, the additional eastern and western gates were removed and blocked up.

Two granaries built in the early part of the third century are the largest surviving internal structures at Birdoswald and are somewhat similar to those found at Corbridge in Northumberland, further to the east. These were large buildings and had raised floors to provide good ventilation for the stored grain. It was during this building phase that the western Hadrianic storehouse was divided off to form several workshops.

When the garrison was scaled down in the fourth century, the original barrack block and storehouse in the north-eastern quarter of the fort was converted into a house for an officer.

The fort was known to the Romans as Banna, meaning 'spur' or 'tongue', and it was occupied by them from AD 122 until about AD 400. It usually housed a garrison of about 1,000 men, and the earliest long-term regiment reputedly came from Romania, although later recruits would have come from Britain. However, the regiment continued to display the curved Dacian sword as a proud symbol of its origin.

Birdoswald carries the distinction of being the only site on Hadrian's Wall at which significant occupation after the Romans left has been proved. The visitor centre tells in detail the intriguing story of the fort and its inhabitants for the last 2,000 years. Excavations and research at the site which took place between 1987 and 1992 suggested an unbroken sequence of occupation on the site of the fort granaries from the late Roman period until possibly AD 500, and further evidence suggests that in the fifth century a local British chieftain built a large timber hall over the collapsed granaries.

Interestingly, the later occupants of the site did not escape the deprivations of the reivers. By the late 1500s the farm at Birdoswald was occupied by the Tweddle clan and there is a record of Hobbe and Robert Tweddle reporting to a muster equipped with padded leather

Storm clouds gather over Birdoswald.

The remains of a defensive corner tower at Birdoswald.

jackets, steel caps and spears, which suggests that they may well have been Border Reivers; although no complaint is recorded against them. However, it is recorded in the Calendar of Border Papers that both of these lodged complaints with Lord Scrope, the March Warden: Hobbe against Old Will Ellot (Elliot), Young Will Ellot and John Ellot for stealing cattle, horses and insight (household goods), and Robert against George Nickson (Nixon) Jenkin Nickson, John Nickson and Eddy Nickson for stealing 26 cows and two horses. The Elliots and the Nixons were among the most notorious Border Reivers.

Recently, a Neolithic burial site has been found, while there is also evidence of a large hall from the Dark Ages on the site. Traditionally, **true** to Cumbrian legend, the site has been identified with Camlan, the site of King Arthur's last battle. More recently, there have been unsettling reports that the modern building is haunted.

Bowness-on-Solway

Bowness-on-Solway is situated in the Solway Coast Area of Outstanding Natural Beauty and to the west of the city of Carlisle. The village has grown up out of the fort that marked the end of Hadrian's Wall and, indeed, many Roman stones have been used in the construction of buildings within the village.

The fort, which they called Maia (translated as 'the larger'), was established to defend the most westerly three-mile crossing point on the Solway estuary. It covered an area of about 7½ acres and was the second-largest encampment on the wall – only the cavalry fort at Stanwix (Petrianum) was bigger. The fort at Bowness was built with its main axis parallel to the sea and the wall itself ran down into the waters of the estuary, past the low-tide mark, in a similar style to that at Wallsend on the Tyne. Nowadays, the only visible signs of the Roman occupation are in a bumpy, unexcavated field opposite the appropriately named Wallsend Guesthouse.

The 12th-century Norman church, dedicated to St Michael, is thought to be built on the site of the fort's granary. The position of the village meant that it was exposed to Scottish raids in the 15th century and it was during one of these forays in 1626 that the church had its bells stolen. Hot pursuit followed and the only way the marauding Scots could make good their escape to Annan on the opposite shore was to jettison the stolen bells. A mysterious tale tells of how they can still be heard chiming at the turn of the tide, deep beneath the waters of the Solway. Retaliation for the theft was swift and

Far left: The 12th-century St Michael's Church is thought to have been built on the site of the granary of the Roman fort.

Far left: The 12th-century St Michael's Church is thought to have been built on the site of the granary of the Roman fort.

Left: A Scottish bell, still in the possession of the people of Bowness-on-Solway.

the aggrieved villagers of Bowness stole the bells from Dornock and Middlebie. The bells are now on display in the rear of the church, on either side of the font. Tradition dictates that every new vicar of the church in Annan requests the return of their bells – only to be firmly, but politely, refused.

A spectacular viaduct was built over the Solway from Bowness-on-Solway to Annan in Scotland in September 1869. This linked the Maryport and Carlisle Railway with the Caledonian Railway at Kirtlebridge and would carry traffic without it having to pass through Carlisle. It was a busy line and over 100,000 tons

The afternoon sunshine illuminates the pulpit in St Michael's Church, Bowness-on-Solway.

The remains of the spectacular Solway railway viaduct just before a winter sunset.

of iron ore were shipped annually from West Cumberland to Scotland. By July 1870 the service was approved to passengers, and although the price of a third-class ticket was fairly expensive at 1s 3d (about 6p), it was somewhat offset by the thrilling experience of travelling over the 1,950-yard viaduct.

The viaduct had 193 spans of girders supported on cast iron columns 30ft apart and stood at a height of 34ft above sea level. Over 2,900 tons of cast iron and 1,800 tons of wrought iron were used and the 12in diameter cast iron piles were driven into the bed of the Solway by piledriver. Interestingly, no scaffold was used and work was carried out from specially constructed barges. The viaduct was designed by Mr James Bunlees, the same man who 10 years previously had built an embankment across Morecambe Bay. Massive embankments were built on both sides of the Solway – 440 yards long on the English side and 154 yards long on the Scottish side – to provide the foundations for the viaduct.

Problems with the viaduct first occurred only six years after its opening, but disaster struck in the winter of 1880. The rivers Esk and Eden had frozen in the upper reaches of the Firth, and when the thaw came great chunks of ice as big as 27 yards square and 6ft thick were carried into the bridge's piers on an ebb tide, travelling at 10 to 15mph. Four watchmen who had been stationed in a cabin in the middle of the structure fled for their lives when the structure started to collapse. They described the sound of the floes hitting the steelwork like that of heavy gunfire, and huge sparks were created as the massive sections of metal fell against each other.

Fortunately there was no loss of life, although 45 of the 193 piers and 37 girders had collapsed. Extensive repairs were carried out and the viaduct continued to be used until 1914. It was not used during World War One but was reopened in 1920. However, by 1922 it was condemned as unsafe and was finally demolished in 1935. It was during this operation that an awful tragedy occurred, when three young men working in a boat at the side of one of the remaining pillars were swept away by a treacherous current. Their boat overturned when it hit a stand of poke nets on the Scottish shore and they were all drowned.

Apparently, part of the reason for the demolition of the viaduct was that the Scots, who then had no access to alcohol on Sundays, used to walk across to the more liberal English side, in spite of the threat of being fined if caught. Unfortunately, one or two returned in a less than sober state and fell into the Solway and were drowned.

Brackenhill Tower, Longtown

Brackenhill Tower at Longtown near Carlisle is an exceptional example of a fortified border tower house and is strategically situated between two deep ravines in the heart of reiver country on the border of the Debateable Lands and the Bewcastle Waste. This type of building is known as a pele tower and was constructed with the emphasis firmly on defence. It has walls almost 2m thick, measures about 10m by 15m in area and is generally three floors or more in height. On the top of the tower is a parapet walkway. This method of construction is called crenellation and allowed the top of the tower to be used as a lookout, but may well also have been used for attack and retaliation during a siege while still maintaining the building's defensive abilities.

The floor of the parapet is one step down, one step up, one step down, one step up, which

Brackenhill Tower once belonged to the notorious Richie Graham – a powerful and much feared Border Reiver.

meant that a defender could see over, or fire from the parapet one second and be hidden from view and protected from returning fire the next, just by stepping onto the next step. Interestingly, there is a peculiarly Scottish detail on the gable of Brackenhill's cap house. The stones running up to the chimney are cut in steps, which are known as crows' steps.

The ground floor of a pele would be used for the storage of goods and livestock, while the upper floors were used as living accommodation. Architectural experts say what makes Brackenhill unique is that it is a Scottish-style tower sitting on English soil and is pretty much intact – even if it is in a precarious position.

It originally dates from the mid-1500s and is strongly associated with the notorious Graham family. It is thought that Fergus Graham of Mote purchased the original house from Sir Thomas Dacre and gave it to his son Richard, or Richie, as he was better known, and it was he who built the present tower in 1584.

Richie Graham was a powerful and much feared reiver, and his expertise in blackmail and protection made sure his fame even reached the court of King James in London. It is widely believed that Richie was the reason why the king singled out the Grahams for special and intense persecution during his 'Pacification of the Borders'.

Richie Graham's great influence, large following and charisma meant that he could put 500 men in the saddle at any one time; however, his reputation, and indeed that of the

Brackenhill Tower, near Longtown, is a fine example of a Scottish-style tower built on English soil.

rest of the Grahams, was less than savoury and the Calendar of Border Papers lists about 60 Grahams as outlaws. One complaint accused them of despoiling over a dozen Cumbrian villages – this was aside from the fights with the Warden's men, harbouring felons and extorting money. It is reported that on one occasion they set fire to Hutcheon Hetherington's house to drive him outside so they could literally 'cut him into collops' (slices).

Brackenhill Tower is, as yet, not open to the public and is on private land; however, it can be seen from the road and a footpath passes nearby. It remains one of the most intriguing border pele towers.

Brough Castle

Brough Castle is an impressive and awe-inspiring sight when approached from Stainmore Pass. It occupies the northern part of what was originally the site of the Roman fort of Verteris. The first stone castle was built here in about 1100 and is thought to have been one of the first stone castles built in Britain. Indeed,

some of the Norman-style herringbone pattern masonry can still be seen. However, by 1174 it had been attacked and burned by the Scottish King William I 'The Lion', and was not rebuilt until the end of the century when Theobald de Valoignes, Sheriff of Lancaster, erected a new four-storey keep on the site of the one that had been destroyed.

In 1268 the castle came into the possession of the Clifford family, and it was Robert Clifford who is credited with building the Round Tower, or the Clifford Tower, in 1300. It was his grandson, Roger, who built the main block,

Brough Castle is thought to stand on the northern part of the site of the Roman fort of Verteris.

The Clifford Tower, at Brough Castle, takes its name from Robert Clifford, who built it in 1300.

including the hall, about 50 years later. The buildings were destroyed by an accidental fire in 1521 and the castle stood derelict for almost 140 years, until it was restored in the mid-1600s by Lady Anne Clifford. After her death in 1676 her successors, the Earls of Thanet, made Appleby their northern residence and Brough fell into a state of neglect, and by 1715 it is recorded that the roof and many of the fittings were sold for £55. By 1763 a lot of the dressed stone of the castle had been removed to provide building materials for several projects, including the building of Brough Mill.

Brougham Castle

Brougham Castle dates from the early 13th century and was built by Robert de Veteripont on the site of an old Roman fort, Brocavum, which guarded an important crossing point on the River Eamont.

By 1268 the ownership of the castle had passed to Robert Clifford, whose father Roger had become Lord of Brougham when he married Robert de Veteripont's great-granddaughter. Robert Clifford became an important figure through his loyal support of Edward I during the Scottish wars, which had started in 1296, and it was he who carried out much of the work at Brougham, improving and strengthening the defences. He was killed in 1314 at the Battle of Bannockburn.

Robert's grandson, Roger, added more domestic buildings in the 1380s, but almost as soon as they finished the castle was captured and sacked by the Scots in 1388.

During the Wars of the Roses Brougham Castle played a key role in the struggle for dominance; indeed, the Cliffords successfully held off a Yorkist invasion until John Clifford was killed in 1461. Brougham Castle then came under the temporary control of the Nevilles, until John's son could reclaim the family estates. Life then returned to a state of relative peace, prosperity and normality for the Cliffords, and in 1525 John's grandson, Henry, was created first Earl of Cumberland.

The last member of the Clifford family to live at the castle was Lady Anne Clifford, who spent the latter part of her long life restoring most of the Clifford properties and spent

Brougham Castle was once a powerful border fortress against Scottish invaders.

Brougham Castle was built on the site of an old Roman fort, Brocavum – the remains of which can still be seen nearby.

several months staying at each in turn, accompanied by her great entourage. Indeed, both James I and Charles I enjoyed the hospitality of Brougham. Lady Anne died at Brougham in 1676 and the Clifford castles became the property of the Earl of Thanet. The earl did not want all the castles and chose to concentrate on his castle at Appleby, and consequently he sold all the furnishings and fittings of his other local castles including Brougham, which rapidly fell into ruin.

Most of the great keep still survives, which was reinforced by an impressive double gatehouse, along with the other 14th-century additions made by the Cliffords when they served as Wardens of the English West Marches, thereby emphasising its importance as a powerful border fortress against Scottish invaders.

Brougham Castle is now in the care of English Heritage. It rests on a low rise beside the sparkling River Eamont, a few miles to the east of Penrith, in what must be one of the most beautiful settings for a castle in all of England. The superb location, however, belies its once turbulent history. The castle's romantic ruin certainly left a great impression on William Wordsworth, who describes in his great work *The Prelude* how he clambered dangerously among the ruins:

That river and those mouldering towers
Have seen us side by side, when, having clomb
The darksome windings of a broken stair,
And crept along a ridge of fractured wall,
Not without trembling, we in safety looked
Forth, through some Gothic window's open space,
And gathered with one mind a rich reward
From the far-stretching landscape.

The imposing keep and gatehouse of Brougham Castle.

Brougham Castle
stands on a
defensive position
overlooking the
River Eamont.

Burgh-by-Sands

Burgh-by-Sands, or 'Bruff', as it is locally pronounced, is a village of mainly 17th and 18th-century houses and is situated on the site of a Roman fort built about AD 95 – they called it Aballava, which translates as 'orchard'. It was originally manned by troops from Holland, Germany and North Africa and was strategically sited to guard two 'waths', or crossing places, on the Solway Firth. The fort was later enlarged to house 500 cavalry troops, who would have been able to deploy much more rapidly than foot soldiers in the face of danger from the north.

The barony of Burgh was created in 1092 to establish a defence against any Scottish incursion from across the Solway. It was first granted to Norman barons such as the D'Estrivers and the Engaines.

Hugh de Morville, who kept back the crowd with his sword while Thomas Becket was murdered in Canterbury Cathedral, once owned the castle here. It is now demolished but the fields where it stood have a typically violent border ring to their names – 'Spill-blood-Holme' and 'Hangman-tree'.

The castle passed through the ownership of the Lucies and the De Multons, to the Dacres and the Howards before it was sold to Sir John Lowther in 1685. His descendents, the Earls of Lonsdale, still hold the title today.

St Michael's Church is thought to stand on the site of one of the main buildings – the headquarters or possibly the granary – of the Roman fort, which of course offered a ready-made supply of dressed building stone. The church received its dedication in the 12th century but the actual construction date is not known. It is safe to say that is built largely in the Norman-style, with much restoration dating from the 1800s. However, the western tower was built in the 14th century.

When Edward I died from the weakening effects of dysentery at Burgh-by-Sands on 7 July 1307, his body was brought to St Michael's and lay in state there for 11 days. His monument on nearby Brugh Marsh is a 19th-century successor to the original memorial erected by the Duke of

The Edward I monument, Burgh Marsh, is a 19th-century successor to the original memorial erected by the Duke of Norfolk in the 17th century.

A rainbow over the Edward I monument on Burgh Marsh.

Norfolk in the 17th century. Edward was a man of great stature and courage, with a powerful and subtle intellect and a genuine and deep love for his people. Many of his achievements are still part of English tradition today. He regarded himself as King of Scotland and was provoked by Robert the Bruce's uprising to embark upon his last war.

He was an imposing and majestic white-haired old man at the time of Bruce's rebellion, but he was so ill that he was transported to Carlisle on a litter, where, with a final furious effort, he mounted his warhorse and rode two miles a day to reach the Marsh at the head of his army.

On his deathbed he told the hapless Edward II to send his heart to the Holy Land with 100

Edward I died on 7 July 1307 and his body was brought to St Michael's, where it lay in state for 11 days.

knights and not to bury his body until the Scots were finally and utterly crushed. He asked that his bones should be carried before the army in the forthcoming campaign so that

There is no arch opening into the tower of St Michael's Church from the nave, instead only a very small doorway guarded by a strong, iron gate or yett, which offered protection during raids by Scottish reivers.

he could lead his forces to victory. Then, with the name of God on his lips, he laid back and died. His passing marked the point in time from which there was constant unrest, trouble, skirmish and war between England and Scotland.

The border is a large area and very difficult to defend. Personal protection was a priority and consequently defensive farmhouses and towers were built all over the area. In rural areas the fortification of church towers was a useful solution and there are three excellent surviving examples in Cumbria, particularly St Michael's in Burgh-by-Sands, with others at Newton Arlosh and Great Salkeld.

The western tower of St Michael's was originally intended to be used as a belfry, but it also had to double as a place of refuge in times of trouble. It has walls about 7ft thick with no access door from the outside, only narrow slits on the ground floor and very small windows on the first floor. There is no arch opening into the tower from the nave, instead only a very small doorway guarded by a strong, iron gate or *yett* offered protection. During raids by Scottish reivers the priest and his villagers would feel secure in the safety of this well-defended building, and, of course, they could ring the bells to attract attention and hopefully get help to relieve their awful plight.

John Stagg, who was born in the village in 1770, became one of the county's most famous inhabitants. He was the son of a local tailor and showed such promise as a lad that it was intended that he should be educated for a position in the church. Sadly, this was not to be as an accident befell him and, blinded, he was forced to scrape a living by selling books and playing the fiddle. During his travels he developed a great understanding of country folk and he expressed this wonderfully in his various volumes of verse. He was as famous in his day as Robert Burns and he is remembered in history as 'The Blind Bard of Cumberland'.

Buttermere

Even the name conjures up a rich, peaceful rural idyll…Buttermere has attracted visitors since Victorian times but some found attractions other than the beautiful, rich landscape of this secluded little valley: they came to admire the grace and beauty of a special local young lady. Mary Robinson was the daughter of the innkeeper in Buttermere village, and her exquisite beauty was made famous by Joseph Palmer in his best-selling book, *A Fortnight's Ramble in the Lakes in Westmorland, Lancashire and Cumberland*, which was published in 1792. Mary became a minor celebrity, and a diversion to the Fish Inn in Buttermere to admire the Maid of Buttermere became an almost necessary part of any visit to the Lake District. She became so well known that she was celebrated by the Lakeland poets, including William Wordsworth, who referred to her as the 'artless daughter of the hills'. However, all did not go smoothly for the beautiful young Mary

and she was tricked into a bigamous marriage by a fraudulent scoundrel – John Hatfield – posing as a Scottish lord. She was completely exonerated of guilt in a sensational trial that resulted in her 'husband' going to the gallows.

The picturesque little chapel of St James occupies a small rise overlooking the village, just at the junction where the roads from over Newlands and Honister Passes converge. William Wordsworth encapsulated the feeling of viewing this attractive little chapel when he remarked, 'A man must be very insensible who would not be touched with pleasure at the sight

'A man must be very insensible who would not be touched with pleasure at the sight of the chapel of Buttermere.' – William Wordsworth.

Mary Robinson, the Maid of Buttermere, was the beautiful daughter of the landlord of the Fish Inn in Buttermere.

A stone tablet is set into the sill of the south window at St James' Church as a memorial to the most famous fell-walker of them all, the great Alfred Wainwright (1907–1991).

and was further restored in 1930. The beautiful local stone from the lower slopes of Red Pike and Sour Milk Ghyll, just across the valley, was used to build the church. Above the porch, added in 1933, is a two-belled tower. The early church congregations were too small to have their own clergyman, so a 'reader', a kind of lay preacher, took the services, and as earthly reward for his efforts he was given free board, lodging, shoes and clothing.

An interesting feature worthy of close attention is the wrought iron 'Shepherd's Gate' at the entry to the porch. It was crafted by Gilbert Hodgson of Warcop in 1968 and serves as a memorial to Revd Geoffrey Orme and Mr Harold Thompson, his brother-in-law.

There is a stone tablet set into the windowsill of the south window near the door as a memorial to the famous fell-walker Alfred Wainwright (1907–1991), who will always be remembered for his seven *Pictorial Guides to the Lakeland Fells*. These little books – handwritten and hand-drawn – are enduring works of art that have fired the enthusiasm of thousands, possibly millions, of fell-walkers over the last half a century. The window looks out on his

of the chapel of Buttermere.' Legend has it that the very first church in the village was a chantry chapel built to celebrate a great victory over Norman invaders by the Saxon Earl Boethar – from whom it is believed Buttermere derives its name. The present building dates from 1840

Buttermere Lake – another beauty of Buttermere.

who hunted mostly on foot, and he also had a reputation as a hard drinker. He formed his own pack, which became famous for its great success.

The now famous song was written by a friend after a day out hunting. Strangely, it was inspired by a lullaby, *Bonnie Annie*, to which tune the stirring words were written. It was first sung at the Rising Sun Inn and immediately became very popular. In 1869 William Metcalfe, the lay clerk of Carlisle Cathedral and also a conductor and composer, wrote new music for the song that saw it achieve national prominence and it eventually became the adopted anthem of the Border Regiment. John Peel's coat of grey, referred to in the song, comes from hodden-grey, a fabric woven from the undyed wool of the local Herdwick sheep of the fells. Peel, whose portraits show him to be cold and hard-natured, died from a fall from a horse on 13 November 1854, aged 78. He is buried in St Kentigern's churchyard and his headstone is elaborately carved with hunting horns and a whip. His fame through the song was so great that there were 3,000 people at his funeral.

The wrought iron 'Shepherd's Gate' at the entry to the church porch was skilfully crafted by Gilbert Hodgson of Warcop in 1968.

favourite place to walk, Haystacks, where his ashes were scattered as his final wish. He remarked, with his wry humour, that 'if a walker gets a speck of dust in his eye on Haystacks – it may well be me!'

Caldbeck

The village of Caldbeck achieved fame because of the song, *D'ye Ken John Peel*:

Yes, I ken'd John Peel, with his coat so gray,
He lived at Caldeck [sic] once on a day,
But now he's gone and he's far, far away;
And we shall ne'er hear his horn in the morning.

It is thought that John Peel was born in 1776 as one of 13 children in Parkend, about a mile from Caldbeck. The mid-17th-century stone building was originally the stables and hayloft to a neighbouring farm but is now a restaurant and hotel. Peel was a well-known huntsman,

John Peel's headstone reads: But now he's gone and he's far, far away; And we shall ne'er hear his horn in the morning.

St Kentigern's Church is dedicated to the saint of the same name, who was thought to have preached here in AD 553 on his journey from Scotland to Wales.

The first building in Caldbeck was probably a hospice for travellers erected by the monks from the priory at Carlisle. However, in the 12th century they built the large St Kentigern's Church, which was dedicated to the saint of the same name, who was thought to have preached here in AD 553 on his journey from Scotland to Wales.

The main fabric of the church is probably Norman, although some of the rebuilding and renovations were completed in the 16th century by John de Wychdale, who was rector at the time. The tower was said to have been added in 1727, but the famed Nikolaus Pevsner disagrees and identifies it as mediaeval. What may solve some of the anomalies he identifies is that the entire church was restored in 1932, when Burma teak beams were added to the roof. St Kentigern and St Cuthbert are portrayed in stained-glass windows. *The last days of Jesus*, an older stained-glass window, dates from the 1800s, as does the clerestory, which is also reputed to be Victorian.

St Mungo's Well, where, it is said, Christians were baptised in the sixth century. St Mungo, of course, is also known as St Kentigern.

Behind the church, near to where the arched stone footbridge crosses the Caldbeck River, lies St Mungo's Well, where, it is said, Christians were baptised in the sixth century. St Mungo, of course, is also known as St Kentigern and was a bishop and evangelist of Strathclyde. It is widely believed that his early teacher, Serf, may have been responsible for giving Kentigern his popular name of Mungo, which translates as 'dear one'.

Mary Harrison, perhaps better known as Mary Robinson or the Beauty of Buttermere, is buried in the same churchyard. Mary lived at the Fish Hotel, Buttermere, and in 1792 when she was about 15 years old she was first noticed by a visitor, Joseph Palmer. He was so taken with the fair maid of Buttermere that he later wrote in one of the very first guide books, *A Fortnight's Ramble in the Lake District*: 'Her hair was thick and long, of a dark brown, unadorned with ringlets, did not seem to want them. Her face was a fine oval, with full eyes and lips as red as vermilion. Her cheeks had more of the lily than the rose.' The publication of this book attracted many tourists to see this famed young beauty. She is mentioned in many of the travellers' diaries of the time and also in writings of the 'Lake Poets', including immortal recognition in *The Prelude* by William Wordsworth.

By the turn of the century Mary was still unmarried and sadly became the innocent victim of a dramatic occurence, which assured her place in the history of Cumbria. In 1802 a gentleman saying he was 'Colonel Alexander Hope', member for Linlithgow and brother to the Earl of Hopetoun, stayed at the inn. He soon courted and won Mary, and, indeed, her parents also took him to their hearts. The couple were quickly married at Lorton church on 2 October 1802. But by 11 October the Keswick correspondent Samuel Taylor Coleridge had published the story in *The London Sun*, and by 6 November 1802 *The London Sun* had quickly discovered that the real Colonel Hope was overseas at the time and that Mary's 'husband' was called John Hatfield, an undischarged

The headstone of Mary Robinson, the Maid of Buttermere.

bankrupt, and he was also married to a lady in Tiverton, Devon. He managed to borrow money from several people in the Keswick area to finance his escape, where first he made for

The Roughton Stone, located in St Kentigern's churchyard, was used to process minerals mined at nearby Roughton Gill and is placed as a monument to the men and their families who worked in the gill for 400 years and who now lie at rest in the churchyard.

Ravenglass to slip on board a ship bound for Wales. He was eventually tracked down and arrested by the Bow Street Runners near Swansea. He was taken to London but the magistrates sent him to Carlisle to stand trial at the local Court of Assize. After an eight-hour trial he was sentenced to death by hanging. His expected reprieve did not arrive and he paid the ultimate penalty. He was guilty of the double crime of bigamy and of false pretences or 'personation', which was considered an extremely serious crime in those days. For a while Mary became famous, but eventually she married Richard Harrison of Caldbeck and together they ran the inn when her parents retired. Later, Richard and Mary moved to Caldbeck, where Mary died on 7 February 1837 a well respected member of the community.

Carlisle

Cumbria has a bloody history, more so perhaps than any other English county, and since Roman times the city of Carlisle has borne the brunt of a lot of it, due, in no small way, to its strategic position close to the border with Scotland. It is possible that Carlisle was a significant defensive site before the arrival of the Romans but there is little trace of earlier settlements; the only evidence is an ancient British ford that once crossed the River Eden a few hundred yards downstream from the main bridge.

The Romans arrived in the area in about AD 80 under the leadership of Agricola. They established a fort, probably constructed from earth and wood, on the site where the cathedral now stands, providing them with a base from which to attack the Scots.

It was the Emperor Hadrian who gave up trying to defeat the Scots and instead established a defensive frontier by ordering the building of his wall in AD 122. Hadrian's Wall stretches from Bowness-on-Solway on the Cumbrian coast to Wallsend, to the east of Newcastle, on the north-east coast. As part of his wall system he ordered a new stone fort, Petriana, to be built in Carlisle at Stanwix, on the north bank of the River Eden. This new fort was the biggest on the wall and was garrisoned with over 1,000 cavalry troops but, sadly, there is now nothing left of what was once the thriving headquarters of the wall system. By the fourth century, however, the civilising Roman influence had greatly declined. Their soldiers were withdrawn from Hadrian's Wall in AD 399 and the last Romans had left Britain by 407. Soon the Roman way of life broke down and many Roman settlements were left to fall into ruin.

What we now know as Cumbria then became part of the Celtic kingdom of Strathclyde. In turn, part of this became the smaller Celtic kingdom of *Rheged* – translated as 'Given Land' – suggesting that the kingdom had been divided between a king of Strathclyde and his son. Around this time, the old Roman name *Luguvalium* was shortened to *Leul* and the Celtic prefix *Caer* – or fort – was added to give the name *Caerluel*, which finally became Carlisle.

We know that Halfdan the Dane savagely sacked Carlisle towards the end of the ninth century and slaughtered every man, woman and child in the settlement and burned every building to the ground. Charred remains of this gruesome tragedy have been found in recent archaeological digs in the city. For over 150 years after this scorching the settlement remained depopulated, scrub vegetation reclaimed the area and it became a group of desolate ruins of little importance. However, in 945 it came under the control of Malcolm, King of Scotland, and remained under his rule until about 1070.

But it was William Rufus, the son of William I, when returning to Carlisle from

It is thought that Carlisle's medieval city walls follow the line of the original Roman bank. William Rufus is reported to have 'set up walls' in 1092 but walls built in stone possibly date from as early as 1130.

Alnwick having just made a peace treaty with the King of Scotland who 'observed the pleasantries of its situation and resolved to raise it from its ruins'. He began work on the castle, established a priory and built the massive city walls. His work was eventually completed by Henry I, who also bestowed cathedral status on the church. However, when he died in 1135 England lapsed into civil war.

Understandably, the Scots still saw Cumbria as being part of their territory and in 1136 King David took the opportunity to overrun and retake the city. He died there in 1153 and during the later years of his reign Carlisle was, effectively, the capital city of Scotland.

The city was in the middle of political turmoil – Henry II of England took the city back but his successor King John lost control of it to King Alexander II in 1216. Finally the city became permanently English under Henry III. By 1293 Edward I of England had succeeded Henry and he granted the town a new Charter but also began to develop the town as a major military base in preparation for his invasion of Scotland. This began almost 400 years of sporadic bloody warfare between the two countries, during which the cruelty and arrogance of the English kings fuelled the wanton savagery of the Scottish leaders such as William Wallace and Robert the Bruce.

King Edward's campaigns of 1298 and 1300 brought an uneasy and delicately balanced peace, but with Wallace's torture and execution in Smithfield and Robert the Bruce's coronation in 1306 in Scotland, the border was again thrown into turmoil.

Henry VIII ordered the strengthening of Carlisle's defences with the construction of two large towers as he was worried about anger at the recent Dissolution of the Monasteries.

Edward I died on Burgh Marsh in 1307 when he was about to lead yet another 'hammering' campaign against the Scots. His son, Edward II, however, was a much weaker leader and Robert the Bruce scored a sensational victory over his army at Bannockburn in 1314 – fired with success he went on to lay siege to the city of Carlisle the following year, and then again, as an encore, in 1332.

Carlisle was not destined, or likely, to become a prosperous city. Its occupants had to be constantly alert against attack and skirmish, there was little time for expansion of commerce and its outlying areas, particularly to the north, became very dangerous places indeed. This was a time when destruction, poverty, hunger and death became a way of life to the ordinary people on both sides of the border. During these years Carlisle fell into a poor state: ravaged by wars, it became little more than a collection of run-down hovels. Any consideration of investment in fine permanent buildings did not materialise because of the inevitable prospect of destruction in the next vicious raid. As well as suffering all the ravages of the Black Death, raids and sieges by the warring Scots followed in 1380, 1385 and 1387, and then a devastating fire in 1391. During the Wars of the Roses the people of Carlisle sided with the Yorkists and ejected the Lancastrian garrison from the castle. As a reward for their loyalty the Yorkist King Edward granted the city a new Charter.

During the reign of Henry VIII the border was comparatively quiet with the uneasy peace between England and France, although it was kept lively through the determined efforts of

the Border Reivers. But in 1541 King Henry VIII closed the priory and two friaries but rebuilt and strengthened the castle – and replaced the southern gate of Carlisle with a citadel with two large towers. He was obviously wary of the Scots and their alliance with the French, with whom he was constantly picking fights. However, reivers and soldiers fought together in 1542 when a large Scottish army was defeated by a smaller English one at the battle of Solway Moss, only a few miles north of the city.

Another severe outbreak of plague struck Carlisle in 1597, in spite of which the population increased until by 1600 Carlisle had a population close to 2,500 inhabitants. During the reign of Queen Elizabeth I in 1568, Mary Queen of Scots was held prisoner in the castle before she was found more secure accommodation in Bolton Castle before being taken south to Fotheringay Castle, where she was eventually executed.

The Civil Wars saw the city firmly on the Royalist side and after York surrendered to Cromwell's Roundheads in 1644, the commander of the King's forces in the north, Sir Thomas Glenham, escaped to the safety of Carlisle.

Again, almost inevitably, the city was placed under siege, this time by an army under the command of a Scottish general, Sir David Leslie. The good people of Carlisle held out for eight months under the gunfire but were reduced to eating horse meat, dogs and even rats; but they still negotiated reasonable terms of surrender. The story has it that when an emissary was allowed to enter the city to discuss terms they gave him so much strong ale that he could hardly stand, and then, convinced that the city still had plentiful supplies, he allowed more favourable terms. However, the city was retaken by the Royalists in 1648 but was recaptured by Parliament almost immediately. Sadly, by this time Carlisle was devastated and its cathedral, walls and houses were in ruins, but mercifully

The market cross, Carlisle, dates from 1682. It was here that Bonnie Prince Charlie was proclaimed King of England and Scotland in 1745.

the end of the war in 1648 brought a few years for much-needed recovery rebuilding. Carlisle was bypassed by the Jacobites in their first rebellion of 1715 but in 1745 Prince Charles Edward Stuart – Bonnie Prince Charlie himself – marched into the city with his Highland army. King James III was subsequently proclaimed from Carlisle Cross but on his return a few months later he was in full retreat and the city was again in Government hands. His campaign marked the end to the constant fight for control of Carlisle.

However, in a border city echoes of a violent past can still return. In 1813 a 15-year-old boy was publicly stripped and whipped and then imprisoned for a month for stealing a handkerchief; bull baiting was still held on the sands until 1824 and a duel with pistols was fought at nearby Kingmoor in 1827.

By the beginning of the 19th century, industry and commerce became more firmly established. The textile trade was confidently prospering and together with brewing, construction, metal box-making and biscuit manufacturing were providing steady employment for a growing population.

The Turf Tavern, Carlisle, was built in 1840 as the grandstand of old Carlisle racecourse.

Tullie House, now an important museum, was originally built in 1689 by the wealthy Carlisle family are from whom it takes its name.

After 10 years of construction, the railway from Newcastle was finally opened in 1838. A canal constructed from Port Carlisle on the Solway Firth led to a very brief period of shipbuilding but it soon closed and was replaced by the dandy railway. It was, in fact, the railway that secured the future of the city – at one time no less than eight busy lines had their terminus in Carlisle, six of which are still in operation. This rapid expansion of industry and increase in population was unfortunately not matched by the rise in standard of quality of life of the inhabitants, and in 1812 living conditions were so bad that large hunger riots took place.

The weavers of Carlisle petitioned the Prince Regent in 1819 in the hope of being sent to America to escape the terrible conditions in which they lived and worked. Things were no better by 1838, however, and another enquiry into their plight was ordered. Conditions were dreadful – people were described as 'huddled in warrens of unsanitary hovels'. Even by the middle of the 19th century there were upwards of 25,000 people with only 5,000 houses to live in, crowded together with animal houses,

The Reivers Cursing Stone was a public sculpture for the millennium, recalling the curse laid on the Border Reivers by the Archbishop of Glasgow, Gavin Dunbar, in 1525.

slaughter houses and communal lavatories, all with open drains running between them. However, during the last years of the century matters did greatly improve when a building programme for hundreds of new houses to the west of the city walls was started.

Since then the balance between commercial progress and general prosperity has been established. The 20th century has been one of continual improvement for the city and its people over the years of harrowing conditions

in the past and previous centuries of war, fire and destruction. Today it has emerged as a confident, energetic city and even its diminutive size adds greatly to its fascinating charm.

Carlisle Castle

Carlisle Castle was renowned as the most formidable fortress on the borders. Even today its massive, brooding red sandstone walls dominate the northern skyline of the city. It was the Romans who first recognised its defensive potential – it has always been one of the main routes into England and needed to be well defended. It was William Rufus who first established a fortification here when he regained possession of Cumberland from Malcolm of Scotland. His castle was probably a wooden tower built on a mound surrounded by a defensive ditch. In 1092 King William II – Rufus – began rebuilding in stone and 30 years later his brother, Henry I, started work on the city walls and built the massive sandstone keep.

Tullie House. Purpose-made delivery bicycles begin with the archetypal 'butcher's bike'. The big front basket may not hold much more in total than you can cram into four panniers on a touring bike, but it will take bigger single items, while smaller packets are easier to get at. This is great for delivering local orders, as the author can testify, after riding such a bike to deliver orders in his father's butcher's business.

Carlisle Castle was renowned as the most formidable fortress on the borders.

King David I claimed the castle for Scotland in 1157 and completed most of the work, before it later fell into English hands once more and Henry II strengthened it even further. It became the focus of regular special attention from the Scots, but with no success – the castle was so strong that it remained impregnable for five and a half centuries.

Edward I made Carlisle Castle his base for his 'Hammering of the Scots' towards the end of the 13th century, and it was here that he held a Parliament with all the due ceremony that would continue as an English tradition. After his death Edward's son was proclaimed king here and received the homage of his nobles.

Carlisle Castle was established as the headquarters for the Wardens of the English West March – this was why the castle's outer gatehouse was built in 1383.

The most determined attempt to take Carlisle was by Robert the Bruce in 1315, and he used every weapon in his armoury, including a new siege engine, and every tactic he knew, but the constant wet weather and miserable flooding was against him and the garrison held firm – having only lost two men. The unsuccessful Scots left after 11 days but not before they had trampled the surrounding cornfields into glutinous mud and driven off all the cattle.

By 1327 the inept Edward II had been deposed and murdered, but his son, Edward III, was a much more accomplished soldier – he learned and sharpened his battle skills against the Scots then applied this experience to great effect against the French. In 1346 the English had decisive victories at the Battle of Crécy and the Battle of Neville's Cross in Durham, where King David was taken prisoner. After this no invading Scottish army ever occupied England again. The king's attention was now focused on the French crown and Carlisle Castle became less important nationally but more important in regional affairs. It was established as the headquarters for the Wardens of the English

West March and it was for this purpose that the castle's outer gatehouse was built in 1383.

The Scots laid siege to Carlisle again in 1385 but were driven back by the newly installed cannon mounted on the keep. By the late 1400s the castle was given a purpose-built gun tower – Richard of Gloucester's tile tower in the south-east curtain wall – which incorporated gun ports in the lower levels to command the lower slopes and was constructed from brick, then a new material favoured for defensive works.

Carvings in the walls on the second floor of the keep were supposedly done with an iron nail by Richard's prisoners, and in the basement dungeon is the macabre 'Licking Stone', which attracted moisture from the air and was used by prisoners in an attempt to satisfy their thirst –

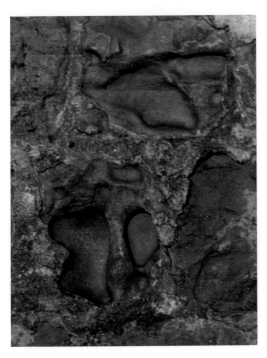

one can still see the deep hollow in it worn by their tongues.

In the early 1500s Henry VIII appointed Thomas Howard, Duke of Norfolk, to Carlisle and he suggested that the castle be further repaired and its armoury strengthened; however, the engineer and builder he employed, Stefan von Haschenperg, was accused of 'spending a lot of money to no purpose'.

Scottish Guns, captured at the Battle of Solway Moss in November 1542, were added to the already well-stocked armoury but in 1547 a huge explosion in the magazine left some big cracks in the walls of the keep. Fortunately, Queen Elizabeth ordered these to be repaired and the fortress strengthened.

In 1568 Mary, Queen of Scots, was brought from Cockermouth and held prisoner for two months until she was found more secure accommodation in Bolton Castle.

In 1596 the castle was the setting for possibly the most dramatic and stirring episode in reiver history – the rescue of Kinmont Willie Armstrong by the Bold Buccleuch, the Keeper of Liddesdale. In the aftermath a furious Queen Elizabeth demanded the surrender of Buccleuch. He appeared before her and she demanded to know how he had dared to carry out such an audacious raid. To which he replied 'Madam, what would a man not dare to do!' The Queen was impressed by his forthright reply and, full of admiration, she is reputed to have cried 'By God! With ten thousand such men our brother of Scotland might shake the firmest throne in Europe!'

After Elizabeth's death in 1603, James VI of Scotland succeeded as James I of England and in the 1600s the City of Carlisle supported the Stuarts – a Scottish army dug in for an eight-month siege in October 1644. Reduced to eating horses, dogs and rats and after hearing the news of King Charles' defeat at Naseby, the Royalists left the city and the Scottish army marched in. They repaired the city walls with stone taken

The carvings on the walls of the second floor of the keep were reputedly done with an iron nail by prisoners held by Richard of Gloucester in the 1400s.

Carlisle Castle dungeons are cold, dark and damp – the prisoners licked moisture from the walls to quench their thirst.

Reiver weaponry on display in Carlisle Castle keep.

from the cathedral and reinforced the castle but were in turn driven out by a Parliamentarian force.

In November 1745 Prince Charles Edward Stuart – Bonny Prince Charlie – and his 'hundred pipers an' all' appeared dramatically on Stanwix Bank to the north of the city and demanded its surrender. He was invading England to claim what he believed was his rightful throne. On his hasty way back to Scotland in December, after the collapse of his efforts at Derby, he garrisoned the castle with a small rearguard. His royal cousin the Duke of Cumberland – the Butcher of Culloden, as he was later known to the Scots – ordered the walls to be bombarded and they were soon persuaded to surrender the 'old hen coop', as he dismissively called the castle! The Jacobite prisoners had little chance of mercy. Some were sent into exile while others were sent to the gallows. The story has it that some of the citizens who had come to watch the executions were so disgusted that they vowed never to attend such a barbaric ceremony again. It is also said that the famous song *The Bonny Bonny Banks of Loch Lomond* was composed by a Highland prisoner in the castle who, by taking the 'low road home' – death – would be in Scotland before his friends who would take the 'high road' – exile.

The importance of the castle began to decline in the regained peace, until the French Revolution triggered discontent and protest among the people of the city. Amid wild rumours of discontent there were corn riots, anti-slavery gatherings and radical protests. The Government responded by building a large armoury in the castle to fight any revolution, and the garrison was made permanent by the construction of the barracks which now fill the outer ward. By 1848 the danger had passed but the troops remained and the military use of the castle continued – the last time guns were mounted on the keep was during World War Two. In 1959 the main body of soldiers moved on but the castle has become the Regimental headquarters with its own museum in the inner ward.

Carlisle Cathedral

The position of Carlisle as a prominent border city is reflected in its dramatic and turbulent

The keep at Carlisle Castle.

history, but its beautiful cathedral is a marked contrast – it is a haven of beauty and peace; although it has still witnessed many dramatic events.

In the south wall arcade of the building is the carving of a head which is thought to be that of King Edward I. On his way to Scotland, in 1307, when he was dying, his litter was dedicated in front of the high altar before starting his last journey to the Solway.

But it was here in 1297 that Robert the Bruce swore allegiance to Edward on the sword that was said to have killed Thomas Becket. The sword which had belonged to Hugh de Morville, a Cumbrian knight, had become an object of great veneration. Interestingly, Robert the Bruce was later excommunicated here.

Although Carlisle Cathedral is the second smallest in England – only Christ Church

Carlisle Cathedral is the second smallest in England – only Christ Church Cathedral, Oxford, is smaller.

Carlisle Cathedral was founded by Henry I and completed in 1102 as a church for the city.

The east window is one of the glories of this wonderful church.

Opposite: The grey section of the original Norman transept and nave, built in the 12th century with stones taken from the Roman wall, which can clearly be seen next to the red sandstone of the later additions to the cathedral.

Cathedral, Oxford, is smaller – it still has a fascinating history and an abundance of interesting features.

It was originally founded by Henry I and completed in 1102, as a church for the city, and then, in 1122 it was made the designated church for the Augustinian order of the Priory of St Mary. It officially became a cathedral in 1133 when Henry created the diocese of Carlisle, and the priory church became the cathedral, the only Augustinian priory church to be so designated.

Although the red sandstone building survived Henry VIII's destructive efforts, it was Oliver Cromwell in 1641 who pulled down much of the west end to build barracks. The chapter house and treasury were turned into a magazine for the garrison. In 1645 Scottish troops destroyed a large part of the nave, reducing it to 200ft – now the shortest cathedral

The early 15th-century oak choir stalls have some notable examples of mediaeval decorative carving and also have some notable examples of decorative mediaeval graffiti!

nave in England – along with the chapter house, dormitory, cloisters and even part of the deanery. The City of Carlisle was originally responsible for its maintenance and upkeep, but they refused to pay for any repairs. In 1745, the Duke of Cumberland used the cathedral as a garrison and Jacobite prisoners were held in the nave. However, large-scale restoration was carried out between 1853 and 1857.

The magnificent east window is one of the more distinctive features and dominates the choir and timber-barrel vault. The intricate masonry was designed by Ivo de Raughton, who was the leading architect of decorative tracery in the north of England and lived only a few miles south of Carlisle.

The upper windows date from the 14th century. The lower nine lights are by John Hardman of Birmingham and date from 1861. They replace the mediaeval windows removed at the time of the Civil War and represent scenes from the life of Christ. There are several other windows by Hardman, including the west window, and the north window in St Wilfred's Chapel. The early 15th-century oak choir stalls and misericords are notable examples of mediaeval decorative carving and have some notable examples of decorative mediaeval graffiti! Behind the choir stalls there are several wonderful ancient painted panels depicting the lives of St Anthony, St Augustine of Hippo and St Cuthbert; tombs; huge flagstones; and two beautiful 16th-century rood screens. The beautiful and ornate Brougham Triptych, found in St Wilfred's Chapel, is a Flemish altar piece and was carved in Antwerp in 1510. The incredible roof is a series of dark blue panels, each with a flaming sun at the centre, and was finished in 1851 by Owen Jones, who decorated the Great Exhibition of 1851. The story has it that when the dean first took a look at it all he could utter was 'Oh my stars!'

On the outside of the nave a carved head commemorates the tragic death in February

Several wonderful ancient painted panels depicting the lives of St Anthony, St Augustine of Hippo and St Cuthbert can be found behind the choir stalls.

Opposite top: The wonderful ceiling, by Owen Jones, is a series of rich blue panels, each with a radiant sun at the centre of its milky way, and dates from 1851. It is said that when the dean first took a look at it all he could say was 'Oh my stars!'

Opposite bottom: The intricate masonry was designed by Ivo de Raughton – the leading architect of decorative tracery in the north of England – who lived only a few miles south of Carlisle.

1965 of a local policeman called George Russell, who was shot and killed at Oxenholme railway station when he was trying to arrest an armed robber travelling south from Scotland.

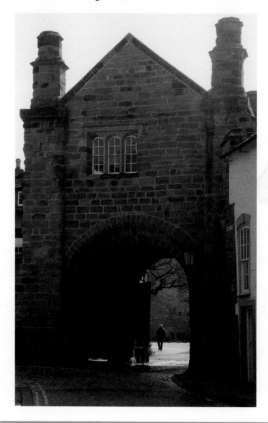

The Cathedral Gatehouse. It officially became a cathedral in 1133, the only Augustinian priory church to be so designated.

Within the cathedral grounds are various other buildings of interest, including the deanery, with its 14th-century Prior's Tower which contains a fine, painted 16th-century heraldic ceiling. The tower was commissioned by Prior Senhouse and serves as a reminder of those dangerous border days when even the clergy had to be constantly vigilant, and indeed prepared, in case of surprise raid or attack.

Carlisle Cathedral has such an excellent reputation that it now welcomes now almost 200,000 visitors a year.

Cartmel Priory

In 677 King Egfrith of Northumbria gave the village of Cartmel to St Cuthbert; however, there is no trace of the remains of these early religious buildings.

It is said that the location of the priory was the result of a vision which inspired St Cuthbert to direct monks from Bradenstoke Priory in Wiltshire to construct a priory between two streams, one flowing north and one south. They

Cartmel Priory has a unique bell tower, the upper part of which was built at a 45-degree angle to its base to house the first bell, added in 1661.

found such a place in the village of Cartmel beside the River Lea and its tributaries. However, another legend tells of how the priory was to be built at nearby Mount Bernard, and it was St Cuthbert who directed the architect to locate the priory between two springs of water; the next morning water flowed from two foundation stones that had been left where the priory church now stands and so this site was chosen. Whatever the accuracy of either legend, in 1188 William Marshall, Baron of Cartmel and later 2nd Earl of Pembroke, founded Cartmel Priory and the Church of St Mary and St Michael in the village for a group of Augustinian canons, which is now considered by many to be one of northern England's finest ecclesiastical buildings.

Not much is known about the priory before the Dissolution. But it is recorded the there were 12 canons serving in the priory plus the lay workforce of 38. Their main purpose was to assist travellers in a safe passage over the Kent Sands because Cartmel was situated right at the northern end of the route. It was especially necessary for travellers to employ a guide to avoid the dangerous quicksand and treacherous channels that changed each day with the fast flowing tides – the graves of people who did not make it across the sands can be seen in the churchyard.

Cartmel Priory suffered extensive damage at Henry VIII's Dissolution of the Monasteries in 1536. Four of the monks and 10 of their supporters from the little farming community steadfastly refused to give up the priory and so were tried for treason and hanged. One notable exception was the prior, Brian Williams, who was awarded a position in the Protestant church. Predictably, the whole of the priory's

The original Priory Gatehouse was built in 1330 and used as a courthouse at the time of the Dissolution of the Monasteries.

property was taken by the Crown and the lead was stripped off the roof, and this helped hasten the building's decay. Also, stone was taken from the walls to use in the construction of other buildings, but the priory survived thanks to its founder, William Marshall, who 350 years earlier had made sure that an altar within the priory was given to the people of Cartmel village and a priest provided for them – taking this into account on appeal the villagers were awarded the right to continue to worship in the church. This right became known as 'unplucked down'. Even though there was no roof, services were still held in the church until 1618 when

George Preston of Holker Hall provided the money for the restoration of the roof. A wide range of building materials, from 12th-century limestone and slate rubble walls to red sandstone, millstone grit and Caen stone, have been used in the construction of Cartmel Priory. The church interior, with its impressive columns, is the result of many centuries of change and improvement, including an enthusiastic Victorian restoration.

Oliver Cromwell stayed in Cartmel in 1643 and used the church as stabling for his troops' horses. The door in the south-west corner of the nave is traditionally called Cromwell's door,

Castlerigg Stone Circle is regarded as one of the most impressive prehistoric monuments in Britain.

where bullet holes and traces of lead can still be seen – allegedly the result of some of the locals taking pot shots at Cromwell's men.

One unusual feature of the priory is its unique bell tower, the upper part of which was built at a 45-degree angle to its base when the first bell was added in 1661; another was added in 1729. The original Priory Gatehouse, built in 1330, was used as a courthouse at the time of the Dissolution of the Monasteries. It is the only survivor of the vast range of original domestic buildings attached to the priory but serves as an impressive reminder of the impact the buildings must have had on any visitor to the priory.

Castlerigg Stone Circle, near Keswick

Every year thousands of visitors flock to this enigmatic site, reflecting on the reason why it was built and, indeed, by whom.

Some of the earliest stone circles in Britain are to be found in Cumbria. There are about 50 and range in type from the huge monumental type like Castlerigg, Swinside and Long Meg to the smaller early Bronze Age circles such as those at Elva Plain and Casterton and, of course, the even smaller examples associated with burials.

Castlerigg is regarded as one of the most impressive prehistoric monuments in Britain and this, combined with its easy access, make it, understandably, the most visited stone circle in Cumbria. Every year thousands of visitors flock to this enigmatic site, reflecting on the reason why it was built and by whom. The site is the flat summit of a low, level hill and affords excellent views across the sweeping landscape to Skiddaw, Blencathra and Lonscale Fell.

Castlerigg is composed of 38 stones arranged in a circle almost 100ft across, and projecting inward from the outer circle is a smaller rectangle of a further 10 standing stones. The stones are of an impressive size and the largest is over 8ft tall. It is thought that the site was constructed about 3,000 BC in the later Neolithic Period. Research has shown that the circle contains significant astronomical alignments, making it an important construction in terms of megalithic astronomy and geology. However, its true origins remain unknown but some historians believe it was used for religious or civil ceremonies.

Whatever its origins, it is an unusual and mysterious site to visit and provides much material for conversation and speculation.

Clifton

The pleasant village of Clifton lies in the attractive vale of Lowther, just over two miles to the south-east of Penrith, near the remarkable outcrop known as Cat Crag which was reputedly, at one time, inhabited by wild cats. Clifton moor is notable as the place where, in 1745, the last battle on English soil took place between Bonnie Prince Charlie's forces and those led by the Duke of Cumberland.

The church, dedicated to St Cuthbert, occupies an ancient place of worship, and legend has it that it is one of the resting places of St Cuthbert's body on its epic journey from Lindisfarne to Durham. He died in AD 687, and after many wanderings avoiding the much feared Viking invaders was buried in Durham – the mighty Norman Cathedral marks his final resting place. St Cuthbert's Church is a small antique building, of the style of architecture which prevailed in the 13th century. A window is dedicated to Eleanor Engayne and displays her family coat of arms. A monument commemorates her marriage. In the 14th century she was mistress of Clifton Hall and a benefactress to the parish. The manor of Clifton was given in the reign of Henry II, by Sir Hugh Morville, one of Thomas Becket's assassins, to Gilbert de Engayne, with whose descendants it continued until in 1364 their heiress, Eleanor, married William de Wyberg of St Bees, in Cumberland. The Wybergs owned the hall during the Civil War and supported the Royalists. They suffered greatly in the Civil War, and one of them, Thomas Wybergh of St Bees, was in the list of delinquents, as they were called, whose estates were ordered to be sold by Cromwell's Parliament in 1652.

Clifton Hall was once a pele tower, then it was developed into a turreted mansion but it now stands at the edge of a farmyard. It was built in the 16th century when the border wars and skirmishes with the Scots had started to become less intense, it was therefore able to have larger windows and be designed more for comfort than defence.

St Cuthbert's Church in Clifton is reputed to be one of the resting places of St Cuthbert's body on its epic journey from Lindisfarne to Durham.

Clifton Tower is good example of a border tower built in the 16th century.

following account may understand. First, as to the rebels, when they came south, we did not suffer much, but they seemed to have great confidence that they would proclaim their King in London, on the 24th of last month, and crown him on New Year's day, and then they would send Geordy, as they called him, over to Hanover, and would tread down his turnip-field dykes; highly dises-teeming the Duke, calling him Geordy's lad and Geordy's Wully, with many more opprobrious speeches; but on their return north, they were cruelly barbarous and inhuman when here, for their leaders gave them liberty to plunder for four hours, and then to burn Lowther, Clifton…and Penrith, and some say for six miles around; but thanks to the Most High, whose power is above the power of man, often preventing wicked designs, it certainly was the Lord's doing in bringing forward the noble Duke and his men in the very hour of great distress; as for my own part, I must ever love and esteem him as a man of worth. Now I shall give thee to understand the beginning and the end of the engagement. First, the rebel hussars being gone past to Penrith, came riding back to my door in haste, between one and two in the afternoon. Then in an hour after, came back again, driving up the rear of their army to my door, and some others then took their place, and they wheeled off and set themselves in ambush against my barn side, being so inclosed with cross houses that our King's men could not see them until close to them, we not knowing their design, but I firmly believed it to be evil, and so went into my house, yet could not long be easy there, and returned forth again, and looking about me, I espied the commanders of the King's men appearing upon the hill, at about 400 yards south of my house, whereupon my very heart was in pain, for believing that a great number might be cut off before they were aware; so our care was to give the King's men notice, for which my son ventured his life, and gave them notice about

Clifton Moor is celebrated in Sir Walter Scott's *Waverley* as the scene of a skirmish in 1745 between the troops of William, Duke of Cumberland and the rebels during their retreat to Scotland, when about 16 were killed on both sides and several were wounded; however, the accounts giving the number slain are very contradictory. A lone tree on a small lane leading from the centre of the village marks the site of the battle and is marked by a poignant plaque beneath its spreading branches.

Thomas Savage, of Clifton End Farm, a worthy member of the Society of Friends, gives the following eyewitness account of the Battle of Clifton Moor:

'By this know thine I received, and shall hereby give thee the results of the affair here, as it was from the beginning to the end. I being both an eye and ear witness to the truth thereof. But in the first place I cannot easily avoid acknowledging the favour and protecting hand of Power to us manifested, as thou, by the

300 yards before they came to the place; when, in the meantime, a second ambush was laid, about 100 yards nearer to our King's men, and the King's hussars, with some of the Yorkshire hunters, came down, and so soon as they came opposite the first ambush, the rebels fired upon them but did no execution; and then issued out the ambush at my doors, and a furious firing they had, the king's men acting quickest and nimblest that ever my eyes beheld, not one of them receiving any harm. Some horse followed the former, so that in a few minutes, the rebels ran away like mad men, and just by my door one of the rebels was brought down and taken, and a Captain Hamilton was also taken at the same time. They were both hard up to the Duke. Then all was still about an hour, in which time I abode in the house, the King's troops still standing upon the common; in which time my son went over a little green to see if he could get the cattle brought into the houses, but seeing that in vain, came homewards again, when four rebels on horseback seized him, calling him a spy, and had him down under their horses' feet, swearing desperately many times they would shoot him; three of them commanded the fourth to shoot him, which he attempted with his gun, and then pistol, but neither would fire, so he escaped and came in a little after. I was again growing uneasy to go out, which I ventured to do, and looking about me, I saw the King's men standing as before upon the common; turning me about, I saw the rebels filling the town street north of my house, and also running down and lining the hedges and walls even down to my house on both sides. Then I was in great pain for the Duke and his men, it beginning to grow darkish; but I ventured my life, and stood a little off, and waved my hat in my hand, which some of them discovering, one of the came riding down towards me, and I called to him, bidding him cast his eyes about him, and see how the town was filled and hedges lined, after which he returned, and then a party was dismounted and sent down to meet the rebels; and, in the time of quietness, as above, they had sent off a party of their horse to plunder and burn Lowther Hall and town, and were also plundering our town, leaving nothing they could lay their hands on, breaking locks, and making ruinous work, even to all our victuals and little children's clothes of

'Here lie buried the men of the army of Prince Charles who fell at Clifton Moor 18th December 1745.'

all sorts. Now, it beginning to grow dark, the rebels were so thick about my house, we had no hopes of saving ourselves, but we concluded on leaving the house, and go into the fields, if we could but get there. In the middle of the orchard we were parted by the rebels, one part of us driven into the fields, and the other part into the house, severely threatening our lives, never expecting to see one another alive again. A son-in-law and his family were under like circumstances, for they seemed more severe upon us then upon others. Now, to come to the matter above again, we were not all got to the fire-side, before the firing, on all hands, was dreadful, which continued half-an-hour, in which time were killed 10 of the King's men and 21 wounded, and the Duke's footman taken prisoner, who was recovered; and of the rebels, five killed and many wounded. Early next morning were 30 prisoners under custody, and after the heat of firing was over, all seemed still a little space, after which some came and broke in at my court door, calling sharply to open; but we believed it to be the rebels, and would not open, when they begun to be sharp, and orders were given to fire, they supposing the house to be full of rebels; but I called, and said I would open as fast as I could, and the first words said to me were "could the Duke lodge here tonight?" To which, with pleasure, I answered "yes". And pleasant, agreeable company he was – a man of parts, very friendly, and no pride in him. Much on his head I could say, if it would not be tedious to thee, and yet I shall mention one thing more to thee, very remarkable, which was, our cattle were all standing amongst the slain men, and not one of them hurt, and them that were banished from our house came in again next morning, which the Duke's men said was a wonder they were not all killed, our next neighbour being shot at the same time. Thou mayest know, also, I had the Duke of Richmond and the Duke of Kingston, with about two more, and as many horse. I have not yet

mentioned a scaffold erected by the rebels, behind a wall, at the corner of my house, as we believe, to cut off any that night coming to my court, which if it had not been that they had fled, the noble Duke had stood a bad chance there. I am afraid thou can scarcely read this; but, if thou thinks proper to show this to anyone, I would have thee copy it fair, and show it whom thou wilt, even if it be to the King, I should be easy, because I know it to be the truth. I will conclude, with true love.'

The Fish Garth and Coop House

During the late 1200s and the early 1300s the River Esk marked the border between England and Scotland. It was generally regarded, and indeed recorded, as a fine river for supplying salmon, and as a consequence of its fame a law was passed saying that no one should be allowed to impede the progress of the salmon upriver to spawn, or the progress of the fry downstream to the sea, by the use of a net or other means placed across the river. Despite the carefully worded regulations, one of the most bitter and long-lasting disputes between the Scots and the English arose because of a fish garth erected by the English to trap the salmon as they swam upstream. This caused a furore with the Scots who lived near the river to such an extent that they entered into a long and bitter feud with their English counterparts. Outraged and claiming they were deprived of a valuable and nutritious food, the Scots took the law into their own hands and destroyed the fish garth.

The grievance and bitter feud rumbled on for years and by 1474 the question was still under heated discussion in London, and eventually a commission was set up in 1475 to try and settle the matter.

The English sent the distinguished figure of the Bishop of Durham to meet with the Scots and he was instructed to explain that the English were perfectly entitled to erect a fish garth and that such a right had been established by custom for the King of England and his subjects. Needless to say the Scots were in strong disagreement.

By 1485 the fish garth had been rebuilt, but it was destroyed again in 1487 by the Scottish borderers and yet another commission was set up. By 1488 the members had agreed that each side should appoint three persons as inspectors of the fish garth. Even this was unsuccessful and in 1490 and 1491 the commission met again to discuss this ongoing problem.

Yet another set of commissioners met in 1494 at the 'Lochmabenstone' on the shores of the Solway to try and 'put a final end to the controversy as to the fish garth' and yet again the English failed to prove their case.

At last, in 1498, a certain amount of progress was made when it was agreed that any damage done to the fish garth should not be regarded as a violation of the peace. And, in the same year, Thomas, Lord Dacre, was granted fishing rights and given permission to construct a fish garth on the Esk by King James IV for a rent of 'four seine of salmond fisch, ilk seine contentand XIIIJ fisch salmond' – at least 100 fish.

Predictably, perhaps, for many years afterwards the English and the Scots eagerly

The Coop House on the River Esk – possibly a store for salmon.

The remains of the fish garth looking west – the fish garth caused a bitter dispute between the English and the Scots.

The Countess Pillar is situated near Brougham.

entertained themselves by alternately rebuilding and destroying the garth – further attempts were regularly made to solve the problem and an uneasy compromise was finally agreed in 1543.

The value placed on the salmon in the Esk was important enough to be included as part of the stakes of single combat which would have been fought between Thomas Howard, the Earl of Surrey, and King James IV before the Battle of Flodden; however, it was suggested that King Henry VIII would not meet the agreed terms no matter what the outcome and so the combat did not take place. They were to have fought for 1. the removal of the Fish Garth and 2. the restoration of Berwick to Scotland.

It is thought that the nearby Coop House was in some way connected with the fish garth – possibly the residence of the person in charge of the fishing (or garthing) or perhaps a place where the salmon were taken and stored after being caught.

The Countess Pillar

The striking Countess Pillar, now on the edge of the main A66 road, marks the place where Lady Anne Clifford, Countess of Dorset, bade farewell to her mother Margaret on 2 April 1616 near the gateway to Brougham Castle. Soon after the parting Margaret died and Lady Clifford erected the pillar in her memory in 1656. Lady Anne was particularly close to her mother who had been her only support during a long inheritance battle.

Lady Anne was born in 1590 at Skipton Castle and was the only surviving child of George Clifford, the 3rd Earl of Cumberland. When her father died his estates went to her uncle but Anne believed the land was rightly hers. Highly intelligent and very determined, she refused to give in over the dispute and after 29 years – in 1642 – she won her struggle.

The unusual sundials on the top of the Countess Pillar.

Her family arms are displayed on the pillar – the Cliffords had owned land in Westmorland, now part of Cumbria, since the 13th century, including the magnificent castle at Brougham and Appleby.

The pillar also carries an inscription stating the wishes of Lady Anne that money should be distributed to the poor of the parish in memory of her mother. A flat stone can be seen nearby

where the alms were distributed on the anniversary of their final parting.

Croglin and its 'Vampyre'

Croglin is an ancient village situated where Croglin Water flows swiftly down from the high, wild, Black Fell. There is a record in the Calendar of State Papers of the village suffering an attack by Scottish raiders in 1346. The original village church dates from Norman times, although the present building, dedicated to St John the Baptist, was constructed in 1878 on the original site.

The village has a tenuous connection with Richard the Lionheart who granted land to a member of one of the old families of the village as a reward for his bravery at the Siege of Jerusalem during the Third Crusade in 1192.

However, the strangest story connected with the village is the tale of the Phantom of Croglin Grange. This is one of the most well known of allegedly true vampire stories in Britain, and occurred before the story of Dracula was written in 1895.

In 1875 Croglin Grange belonged to the Fisher family, whose ancestors reputedly had connections with the Knights Templar in the Holy Land. The family moved from the Grange into a larger property and put the house up for rent. During the long, cold winter the house stood empty but in the early spring it was rented to two brothers and a sister who went by the name of Cranswell. They settled quickly into village life and routine and soon became popular members of the community.

Late one summer evening, after the brothers, Michael and Edward, had retired to bed, Amelia, their sister, stood gazing at the lengthening shadows in the nearby graveyard when her attention was attracted by two burning points of light above one of the gravestones. In time they moved silently across the graveyard and seemed to approach the house. She panicked, closed the open window and tried to leave the room but it was too late – the points of light materialised into the red eyes of a demon-like creature, which was scratching at the window panes to try and get in. Amelia tried to scream but abject terror froze the sound in her throat. The window slowly opened

The sinister, moonlit churchyard, near the Grange.

Croglin churchyard in gathering clouds.

inwards and a figure climbed through the gap with swift, cat-like ease. Amelia could now hardly breathe as the towering figure of a pale, almost translucent man with burning eyes and blood-red mouth stood over her. He grasped her hair in one movement and pulled her head back to deliver a savage kiss to her exposed neck. At last she found her voice and the high, blood-curdling scream awoke Michael and Edward who were sleeping in nearby rooms. They were at her door almost instantly, breaking it open with a heavy poker to gain entry, and they were greeted by a dreadful sight – their sister lay on the bed with blood pumping from two dreadful punctures to her throat and the room was heavy with the awful, heavy choking stench of mouldy decay. They glimpsed the creature escaping through the window and across the countryside to the fells above the house. The brothers managed to stop the loss of blood and revive Amelia and the next few hours were spent in the attempt to save her life.

Amelia eventually recovered her strength and her brothers took her to Switzerland to recuperate in the clean mountain air. Michael and Edward swore revenge on the creature and when Amelia heard of the plan she persuaded her brothers to let her act as bait for the dreadful creature. They agreed in spite of many misgivings and eventually the Cranswells returned to Croglin.

Once more Amelia took up her position in the bedroom. Once more the awesome figure entered the room but this time the brothers were lying in wait with pistols and as the creature slid through the window they fired at point-blank range. The creature let out an unearthly scream and fled into the night. Rather than follow in the dark the two brothers got their sister to safety and at first light gathered all the residents of the village to help find the beast. They searched the graveyard but found no signs and so turned their attention to the church. The crypt door was open and they made their way into the gloom. All around were the remains of damaged coffins and the grisly remains of their contents, but one coffin stood in the corner apparently untouched by the carnage. They quickly heaved off the lid and were faced with a hideous grey body in mouldy clothes and with a fresh bullet wound gaping in one of its legs – the men wasted no time and dragged the coffin out into the churchyard where they quickly burned it to ashes. The dreadful Croglin Bat has not troubled the village and its inhabitants since…well, up to now…

Crosscanonby Salt Pans

In Anglo-Saxon times there was no refrigeration and the only way to preserve foods such as fish or meat was either by smoking or salting – the latter was the most popular method, and, of course, the preferred method of preserving hides and skins, making salt a highly prized and valuable commodity. Its production in Cumbria made it the third most important industry behind agriculture and fishing; indeed, salt was wanted in vast quantities by the local fishing industry and so salt production was carried out on a large scale throughout West Cumbria, with an almost unbroken chain of salt pans stretching from the head of the Solway Firth right down to the fishing village of Holborn Hill, or Millom, as it is now more familiarly known.

The Crosscanonby salt pans are probably the best-preserved examples of salt works in West Cumbria. The earliest known reference to Crosscanonby salt pans was in 1634 when they were let to a gentleman by the name of Richard Barwis on a 21-year lease, the details of which show plans for the construction of salt pans and the building of nearby cottages. The ownership of the pans passed to the Lamplugh family from Ribton in 1662, first to Thomas Lamplugh and then to his son, Richard, in 1670. From then on they were a source great disagreement in the Lamplugh family. The two half-brothers, Richard and Robert, both sons of Richard Snr, argued extensively over ownership in 1710, but it was the very wealthy Robert who was eventually awarded the lease by the Dean and Chapter of Carlisle Cathedral. The last lease to mention the salt pans was granted to one Joseph Fell of Crosscanonby in 1821, although it is generally thought that salt production on the site actually stopped in the 1760s.

The pans were large, circular elevated structures called sleech pits or kinches. These were made of cobbles and had a clay-lined floor

The Crosscanonby salt pans are thought to be the best-preserved examples of salt works in West Cumbria.

The Cumbrian coast was one of only six areas in Britain where salt was taken from the sea.

covered with reeds to act as a filter. Horse-drawn wagons would bring salt-laden sand from the shore and this was loaded into the pan and liberally doused with water. A strong salt solution would leach to the bottom and this was then gently boiled in iron pans. These were about 9ft by 8ft and could be up to 8ft deep and sat on stone pillars to allow space for the fire to burn underneath.

'Panwood', which was actually a poor-quality coal of no commercial value, was used to fuel the fire. Once the brine was simmering, buckets of animal blood, obtained from the local slaughterhouse, were added to the simmering solution. Although this produced a dreadful disgusting liquid, the albumen in the blood acted as a coagulant – in the same way that a white of an egg can be used to clarify wine. When the albumen in the blood thickened and congealed it formed a thick scum that absorbed all the impurities and floated on the surface – it could then be scraped off with a wooden rake.

When all the water evaporated the remaining salt crystals were removed with wooden shovels to prevent damage to the steel pans. The salt crystals were then loaded into wicker baskets for transportation and sale. This method would only yield about three per cent salt as this is the normal percentage of salt in seawater.

Because the workers were not allowed to work on Sundays, the highly prized 'Sabbath Salt' was produced on Mondays from the previous Saturday's brew. This had larger crystals because the brine was allowed twice the time to evaporate and, naturally, it commanded a higher price, which would compensate the panmasters for the loss of production on Sundays.

However, the mid-18th century saw a sharp decline in the demand for salt. Winter fodder such as turnips and mangel-wurzel became readily available and so farmers no longer needed to slaughter large quantities of animals in the autumn for the meat to be pickled or salted – fresh meat was now available all year round.

The salt pans are now regarded as a unique and valuable monument to a once thriving industry because the Cumbrian coast was one of only six areas in Britain where salt was taken from the sea.

St Andrew's
Church, Dacre, is
thought to have
been built on the
site of a Saxon
monastery.

Dacre and the Bears

The ancient parish of Dacre has had a church on
the same site for over a thousand years. It was
mentioned as early as AD 731 by the Venerable
Bede in his *Ecclesiastical History*, and hosted a
meeting of the kings of Strathclyde, Scotland
and England in the 10th century. There is no
trace of the Saxon monastery where the three
kings met, but the Norman church is believed to
be built on or close to the site and, indeed, is
thought to be built with stone reclaimed from
the monastery, which, in turn, was probably
built with stone taken from a Roman camp
which originally occupied the site.

The four corners of the graveyard are
marked by four famous carved stone bears,
known as the Dacre Bears. They provide much
material for speculation but in reality not much
is known about them, although some historians
believe they do tell a story. Bishop Nicolson,
writing in 1704, linked the bears to the chained
bear and ragged staff on the arms of the Earls of
Warwick; however, these two emblems were not
actually used together until mediaeval times
and the church and bears appear to be much
older.

In 1890 Chancellor Ferguson studied the
bears closely and put forward the following
theory. He suggested that they were a humorous
rendering of a bear legend. In the first carving,
a bear stands alone. In the second one an
animal attacks the bear from behind. And in the
third the bear and the creature grapple. The
fourth and final carving shows the bear by itself
with a satisfied smile on its face, suggesting that
the bear has eaten the mysterious animal! The
tale may seem a strange one for a churchyard,
but it has been suggested that the bear and
creature represent religious ideals in the story.
The truth is that nobody really knows what the
statues represent, and the speculation
undoubtedly adds to their appeal.

However, the 'smiling bear', which is in the
best state of preservation, seems to have a mane

*The four corners of
the graveyard are
marked by four
famous carved
stone bears, known
as the Dacre Bears.
These mysterious
creatures provide
much material for
conjecture and
speculation.*

The Viscount William Whitelaw Memorial Window, situated in the south aisle of St Andrew's Church, Dacre.

Dacre Castle was built by William Dacre and his son Ranulph sometime during the 14th century as a pele tower for protection against Scottish raiders.

and a long tail which does not suggest a bear but a lion – indeed, some historians have suggested that the 'bears' are really lions. Another recently expressed archaeological opinion is that they are pre-Saxon in origin and may possibly have marked boundaries of some pagan sacred site.

Dacre Castle, situated not far from the church, was built by William Dacre and his son Ranulph sometime during the 14th century as a pele tower. These fortified houses were not built to withstand prolonged siege but as a place to offer short-term protection for border landowners, their stock and tenants from raids and incursions by the Scots.

The castle fell into disrepair but was restored in the 1670s by the Earl of Sussex, who turned it into a private home at great and extravagant expense. When he died his lavish lifestyle left his widow and children impoverished and so the

Far Left: A mortice lock and key on the south aisle door dated 1671 that was presented by Lady Anne Clifford as Anne, Dowager Countess of Pembroke.

castle was purchased by Sir Christopher Musgrave who eventually sold it, in 1723, to his future son-in-law, Edward Hassell of Dalemain, whose descendants are still the owners. It stood neglected until 1960 when it was let to be renovated.

The castle is reputed to be haunted by a former owner's wife and her lover, whom the owner murdered in a fit of jealousy.

Dalton Castle

In 1127 King Stephen granted Furness Abbey the right to administer justice in the Dalton area. It was not long before marauding Scots

Left: The Victorian Drinking Fountain in Dalton.

destroyed the abbey buildings that had served as a centre of administration, and so Dalton Castle, in reality a much better fortified pele tower, was built in the mid-1300s as a replacement complete with courtroom and a prison.

The castle had 6ft-thick walls at ground level and further protection was afforded by an easily defendable spiral staircase built in to the west wall, which allowed access to the two upper floors and the crenellated roof.

On the nearby market square is a striking Victorian drinking fountain, with beautifully fluted columns supporting a dome of open ironwork. Next to it is the market cross surrounded by 19th century stone slabs for fish drying.

Duddon Iron Furnace

Duddon Iron Furnace has to be one of the most impressive charcoal-fired blast furnaces in Britain. The first blast furnace in the area was

Dalton castle was built in the mid-1300s as a defensive pele tower.

The charging house at Duddon Iron Furnace.

built in 1711 in Backbarrow, and Duddon Iron Furnace was built in 1736 by the Cunsey Iron Company and used the abundant local supplies of iron ore, charcoal and water. The furnace worked until 1867 with few alterations to its original design. Between 1711 and the late 1740s eight blast furnaces were built in the area, and the constant demand for charcoal meant that each furnace drew supplies from vast areas of coppice woodland. For example, the furnace at Duddon needed the charcoal produced from 10 acres of woodland every week.

Iron ore had been mined in Furness and West Cumbria from the Middle Ages onwards, and smelted in primitive hearths or bloomeries, usually in places where large amounts of charcoal were easily available. But it was in the 18th century that blast furnaces revolutionised the smelting process. Large furnaces were built, consuming large amounts of ore and fuel, and harnessing water power to drive bellows which blew air into the combustion chamber. A blast furnace is a type of metallurgical furnace used for smelting to produce metals, generally iron. The charcoal and iron ore were heated together to a temperature of 1,500 degrees C, using the

The wheel pit at Duddon Iron Furnace.

water-driven bellows to increase the intensity of the fire, and the carbon combined with the oxygen in the ore leaving pure molten iron and slag. Fuel and ore would be continuously supplied through the top of the furnace, while air was forced into the bottom of the chamber,

Duddon Iron Furnace's casting arch.

remaining two men – one known as the 'keeper' and the other as the 'founder' – were involved in casting the pig iron.

Coal was considered as a possible alternative to wood, and although it was cheap it was found to be unsuitable for making iron because of its sulphur content – this made the iron too brittle to be any good. However, in the early 18th century Abraham Darby successfully smelted iron using coke as fuel – it is said that he was so overjoyed with his discovery that he bought beer for all his workers at his furnace. Some historians believe he even passed his tabs round.

And so, when coke replaced charcoal as the source of carbon, these rural furnaces became obsolete. Duddon stopped producing iron in 1867, although the buildings remained intact until the early 1900s. The site was declared a scheduled ancient monument in 1963 and in the early 1970s extensive restoration was carried out by Cumberland County Council.

Egremont

The small market town of Egremont was once the scene of bloody conflict with invading Danes, and lies a few miles inland from St Bees on the bank of the river Ehen, flowing seaward from Ennerdale. Its name probably originates from the town of Aigremont in Normandy, and is translated as 'Mount of Sorrow'.

Egremont market first started in 1267 when King Henry III granted a Charter to Thomas de Multon, and the tradition of the Crab Fair, also first held in 1267 when Lord Egremont gave away crab apples, still continues. On the third Saturday in September, during the 'Parade of the Apple Cart', apples are still thrown to the public. Track and field events, shows and hound trails take place. One of the earliest events was the prize of a sheep fastened to the top of a greasy pole and anyone who was able to climb to the top took the prize; today it is a leg of lamb

so that the chemical reactions took place continuously throughout the furnace as the material moved downward. The end products of the molten metal and slag were tapped from the bottom, and flue gases extruded from the top of the furnace. Production would run continuously for periods ranging from 20 to 30 weeks, and around 10 tons of iron would be drained off every 12 hours into moulds and made into the ingots known as pigs. These products of the furnace were then taken away by barge to Chepstow or Bristol where they would be used in the manufacture of chains, anchors and other ships' fittings.

Although many men were needed to produce the vast quantities of charcoal and iron ore needed for production, it only took six men on each shift at Duddon to keep the furnace working.

Two men – the 'bridge servers' – kept a steady supply of iron ore and charcoal going to the Bridge Loft where another two men – the 'fillers' – weighed the charge and filled it into locally made swill baskets and tipped it into the mouth of the furnace. In the casting house the

Egremont Castle and the old market cross.

On a mound above Egremont's main road are the Cumbrian red sandstone ruins of a castle built around 1120 by William de Meschines and once the seat of the barony of Copeland or Egremont. Egremont was too far south of the border to be affected by the usual reiver activity, but in 1315 Robert the Bruce and Lord James Douglas drove deep into Cumberland, attacked Egremont and spoiled the priory at St Bees. It was on this raid or the subsequent one in 1322 that Calder Abbey also suffered severe damage. Through the following centuries the castle passed through numerous hands including William Fitzduncan – a nephew of David I of Scotland – the Earl of Sussex, the 15th Earl of Northumberland and the Crown.

that the climber claims. A famous and unusual aspect of the fair is the World Gurning Championships, where men and women put their heads through a horse collar and 'pull faces', with the worst, or best, depending on your point of view, made World Champion!

Norman Nicholson, the respected Cumbrian poet, once wrote 'the stone of the castle is dark and sullen. Much blood has soaked into it' and in his poem *Egremont* he says:

Of pillage, plunder, famine, fear
Still the moated dungeons hide
Legends of poverty and pride
And murdered skulls are stuffed with lore

The eerie ruins of Egremont Castle.

And dirk has carved upon the bone
Blood will not show on the red stone.

There are numerous legends about Egremont and it is Parson and White who, in their *History and Gazetteer of Cumberland*, recall the traditional story of Lady Eleanor Lucy, who was attacked and devoured by a wolf while walking near the castle one evening. The place, named Woeful Bank, is now marked by a cairn of stones.

In about 1204, Richard Lucy held the position of Forester of Cumberland. The badge of the forester was a bugle horn and the story of the 'Horn of Egremont' probably came from this: Two brothers rode off to war; the eldest was taken prisoner and held for ransom while the younger was sent home to raise the necessary money. When he arrived home he decided to do nothing and takes his brother's place. The elder brother, however, unexpectedly gained his freedom through the love of his captor's daughter. He returned to blow the horn hanging by the castle gate – which only the true heir could sound – and regained his rightful position.

In 1806 William Wordsworth wrote a poem called *The Horn of Egremont Castle* in which he tells a variation of the tale:

Hubert set off on one of the Crusades and as
true knights they showed their mettle:
Side by side they fought (the Lucies
Were a line for valour famed)
And where'er their strokes alighted
There the Saracens were tamed…

But Hubert becomes envious and arranges to have his brother murdered:

'Sir' the killers say to Hubert
'Deep he lies in Jordan's flood'

With this assurance Hubert rides home and assumes the position supposedly left vacant by Sir Eustace. But Sir Eustace is not dead as reported and rides home, sounds the horn and reclaims his position. Hubert begs forgiveness and enters a monastery.

Curiously, Walter Fitzwalter, while he was Lord of Egremont, was captured while fighting in France and had to mortgage the castle to raise his ransom.

Wordsworth immortalised another Egremont legend in his *Boy of Egremont*, about William Fitzwilliam: The boy's father is a cruel and vicious man, who leads raids across the north of England, pillaging and plundering and murdering and torturing men, women and children. On the father's death, the son – the Boy of Egremont – inherits the Earldom of Moray and much of northern England. He is eventually raised to the position to become King of Scotland, but meets untimely death through an unexpected and tragic accident while out with his dog. A forester says that the boy tried to leap across a chasm in the River Wharfe, misjudged it and plummeted to his death. However, the body was never recovered, so the story remains a mystery…

The Florence Mine at Egremont once supplied the foundries at both Workington and Whitehaven with haematite iron. The miners were traditionally nicknamed 'The Red Men of Cumbria' after the red colour of the iron ore they became stained with during their work. Metal mining in the west of Cumbria was dominated by the large deposits of high grade hematite iron ore found in the limestone strata. To the north of the mining field some of the

Haematite Miner *by Colin Telfer.*

Railway trucks at the Florence Mine.

deposits were found to outcrop and it is possible that this was first exploited by the Ancient Britons and almost certainly by the Normans in 12th century.

Mining flourished from about 1830 with the advent of new technologies used in iron and

The Florence Mine.

steel making where a high grade ore with low phosphorous levels was preferred. The depressions of the 1920s and exhaustion of shallower deposits finally closed most of the mines, and Florence Mine was the last to close in 2006 when it held the distinction of being the last working iron ore mine in Western Europe.

The mines are famous for their superb sea-blue fluorite crystals on creamy coloured dolomite; although examples of green and purple fluorite are also found. Also, clear cubes with varying shades of brown caused by hematite inclusions form attractive specimens which are usually associated with dolomite and barite. 'Kidney-ore' was often found in large specimens and both clear and smokey samples of quartz made particularly pleasing aesthetic pieces. In the early 1990s there was a most unusual find of white spheroidal calcite on specularite.

The Florence Mine provided an opportunity for visitors to gain some idea of this traditional local industry but sadly a decision by the owners, BNFL, to no longer cover the costs of pumping water out of the mine brought about its final closure.

Fox's Pulpit

High on Firbank Fell between Sedbergh and Kendal is a high, rocky outcrop known as Fox's Pulpit. It was here in 1652 that George Fox addressed a multitude of pilgrims and thus began the Quaker movement, or the Society of Friends. The commemorative plaque on the rock reads: *Let your lives speak. Here or near this rock George Fox preached to about one thousand seekers for three hours on Sunday 13 June 1652. Great power inspired his message and the meeting proved of first importance in gathering the Society of Friends known as Quakers. Many men and women convinced of the truth on this fell and in other parts of the Northern Counties went forth through the land and over the seas with the living word of the Lord enduring great hardships and winning multitudes to Christ. June 1952.*

George Fox was the son of a prosperous Puritan weaver in Leicestershire and was originally apprenticed to a shoemaker in about 1635. However, he was continually troubled by periods of melancholy and religious torment, which led him to take up an itinerant life as a travelling shoemaker. He travelled around Leicestershire, Derbyshire and Nottinghamshire talking to clergymen and others religious figures searching for spiritual guidance. Unable to find satisfaction for his religious needs, he broke away from the established church.

In 1647, Fox experienced a spiritual vision which convinced him that all earthly authority was corrupt; God's message came to individuals directly through the inner light of their personal inspiration. Fox broadcast his message as he travelled around the Midlands and North, attracting small

George Fox addressed a multitude of pilgrims at this windswept place in 1652 and thus began the Quaker movement, also known as the Society of Friends.

High on Firbank Fell between Sedbergh and Kendal is a rocky outcrop known as Fox's Pulpit.

groups of followers who called themselves Friends of the Truth.

Fox's denunciations of the established church and its ministers upset the authorities and this led to his imprisonment in Nottingham in 1649 and in Derby from 1650–1651. During his imprisonment in Derby, Fox was offered a chance to gain his freedom by joining the army raised against the invasion by Charles II and the Scots; but he stood by his principles and refused. Pacifism was to become an important belief throughout the Quaker movement.

After he was released towards the end of 1651 Fox resumed his religious calling in Yorkshire and Lancashire. He called for the abolition of tithes, refused to accept social superiors and wholeheartedly insisted that anyone, including women and children, could speak at Quaker meetings.

After he experienced divine guidance on Pendle Hill in June 1652, he travelled to Firbank Fell near Sedbergh where he addressed a gathering of over 1,000 people. Among the many disciples convinced by Fox's preaching during this period was Margaret Fell (1614–1702), wife of Thomas Fell, a prominent magistrate. Margaret Fell became the chief organiser of the Society of Friends and married George Fox after the death of her husband.

The Quaker movement spread to southern England during the mid-1650s. When Fox came to London in March 1655, he was personally interviewed by Lord Protector Oliver Cromwell who was impressed by his plain speaking and religious sincerity. Despite Cromwell being sympathetic to their views, many Quakers were still imprisoned by local magistrates for causing disturbances through their beliefs.

Nowadays, in all, there are about 210,000 Quakers worldwide. In Britain there are 17,000 Quakers, and 400 Quaker meetings for worship each week. About 9,000 people in Britain regularly take part in Quaker worship without being members of the Religious Society of Friends.

Furness Abbey

Furness Abbey, or St Mary of Furness, is a former Cistercian monastery situated on the outskirts of Barrow-in-Furness. It was founded in 1123 by Stephen, Count of Boulogne and Mortain and Lord of Lancaster, and was originally built for the Order of Savigny from Normandy in northern France. The abbey is located in what is known as the 'Valley of the Deadly Nightshade' that lies between Dalton-in-Furness and Barrow-in-Furness, and is built entirely out of the attractive local red sandstone.

Furness Abbey is located in the 'Valley of the Deadly Nightshade' that lies between Dalton-in-Furness and Barrow-in-Furness.

In 1147, despite much protesting, it was transferred to the Cistercian Order of Monks, who gradually enlarged and rebuilt the original church. Most of the ruins that can be seen today date from the 12th and 13th centuries and by the 15th century it had been almost rebuilt and had become the second richest – after Fountains Abbey in Yorkshire – and one of the most powerful Cistercian abbeys in Britain.

For many years the abbey enjoyed the position of being the only religious house north of the Mersey and west of the Pennines. Consequently its possessions were vast – it owned land in Yorkshire and as far away as Ireland. All through the Middle Ages Furness and Fountains continually disputed their holdings in Cumbria but the rights, and indeed the privileges, of Furness Abbey were confirmed and extended by every king from Henry I to Henry IV, and in 1134 King Olaf of the Isle of Man granted land to Furness for the foundation of a daughter-house and the right to elect a bishop of the Isle of Man. The abbey of Furness enjoyed a great amount of independence in the north of England and the abbot was almost regarded as a border baron

by the neighbouring Scots; only the King of England could stand in the way of the abbey's influence in the North West. The abbot was also an important person at the king's court. When the king progressed north the abbot collected subsidies, assisted the royal officers

Most of the ruins of the abbey that can be seen today date from the 12th and 13th centuries.

and judges, and acted as arbitrator and meant that he quite often became involved in local disputes. For instance, in 1357 one Thomas of Bardsey in Ulverston is reported to have seized the abbot's bailiff, Roger Bell, and beat him while he was carrying out his duties. After the attack, the bailiff returned with a company of men, including Abbot Alexander, to avenge the insult only to find that Thomas had barricaded himself into his father's house. The Bailiff and the monks attacked the house and smashed down the door. Thomas was duly captured and carried off to gaol in Dalton – a firm assertion of the might and justice of the abbot.

The close proximity of the abbey to the Scottish border meant that it suffered many raids from the marauding Scots during the course of its long and eventful history. It was attacked in 1316 and again in 1322 by the rampaging army of Robert the Bruce.

The late mediaeval bow bridge over Mill Beck.

The abbot, John Cockerham, agreed to pay a ransom to the Scottish king and even entertained him in his own lodgings rather than trying to defend the abbey and its property. The Scots accepted the abbot's hospitality and the ransom money, but still took the opportunity to sack and pillage the surrounding countryside and its settlements.

Furness was a remarkably wealthy abbey; in the survey of 1535 the net annual income was valued at over £800 which made it the second richest Cistercian house in England, and as such it should not have been dissolved until 1539 when the larger monasteries were forced to surrender. Unfortunately, some of its monks were heavily involved in the ill-fated uprising known as in the Pilgrimage of Grace during the winter of 1536; this meant Furness had openly questioned Henry VIII's declaration of supremacy over the church and led to its early closure in 1537. When the king's agent and

close friend, Robert Radcliffe, rode north to quell the resultant disturbances of 1537, marking his progress with a series of selected executions, he suggested that Furness should surrender as a 'voluntary discharge of conscience'. The abbot, Roger Pyke, agreed immediately. Demolition began almost at once, the lead from the abbey roof was stripped and melted down and the site and lands were forfeited to the Crown. The property remained in private hands until 1923 when Lord Richard Cavendish placed the abbey into the hands of the Office of Public Works. It is now cared for by English Heritage.

These romantic ruins are now a popular tourist attraction and lie on the Cistercian Way, a new footpath that follows an ancient track which used to link the abbey with the nearby town of Dalton-in-Furness, which crossed the late mediaeval stone bridge over Mill Beck that can still be seen nearby. Also the ruins are undoubtedly a great inspiration to the arts. William Wordsworth visited here on a number of occasions and referred to it in *The Prelude*, his famous auto-biographical poem written in 1805, and William Turner the celebrated artist made numerous etchings and drawings of the abbey. Naturally, such an evocative place is linked with a number of legends; a tunnel is said to run from the abbey to both Piel Castle and Dalton Castle, allowing the monks to travel to and from each fortification in safety. There is also a rumour that the Holy Grail and King John's long-missing crown jewels are actually hidden somewhere inside the abbey. And, naturally, there are a couple of stories of how Furness Abbey is haunted, both by a beautiful but sinister white lady and a headless monk on horseback, who cannot see where he is going...

Gamelands Stone Circle

About halfway between the villages of Orton and Raisbeck is a trackway leading past one of the largest stone circles in Cumbria. This is the ancient Neolithic or early Bronze Age Gamelands stone circle which is about 100 yards in circumference. Unfortunately its stones, all of them pink Shap granite except one, which is limestone, have fallen, and none of them is any higher than about 3ft, so it is infrequently visited, although access is easy. Although it would appear to have been partially

Gamelands is one of the largest stone circles in Cumbria.

Gamelands stone circle is strangely beautiful in its dramatic setting.

destroyed, it is still easily recognisable. The circle is in fact oval shaped and measures about 50ft by 40ft and is built on a low bank, and it is possible that it once had a central burial cist. It is in an attractive and peaceful setting with excellent and extensive views. The circle once had 40 stones but Victorian farming with its disregard for preservation has both damaged and reduced them and there are now only 33 stones left. The monument is officially classified as a flattened and embanked stone circle. Situated close to the base of Knott Scar, artefacts have been found here that are thought to date from the period between 1800-1400 BC.

There are over 1,000 stone circles in Britain of different designs and construction but their presence provides much material for speculation and contemplation.

Despite the damage, Gamelands is still worth seeing – it is strangely beautiful in its dramatic setting.

Gosforth Cross, St Mary's Church, Gosforth

The famous 10th-century Gosforth Cross is situated in St Mary's churchyard between the main door and the entrance to the churchyard. It is the tallest Viking Cross in England and regarded as the second most important example after the Bewcastle Cross. This tall and slender red sandstone cross stands at a height of about 14ft with a round shaft at the base which gradually becomes square higher up. The cross is decorated with well preserved elaborate carvings which are said to represent figures from Norse mythology such as Thor, the god of sky, thunder and fertility; Loki, the sly, trickster god; and Heimdall, the watchman of the gods. The lower rounded part of the cross is thought to represent Yggdrasil, the Viking World Tree, a great ash tree, which according to Norse beliefs

Far left: The famous 10th-century Gosforth Cross is the tallest Viking Cross in England.

Left: Detail of the Gosforth Cross.

was the very centre of the universe. One of the carvings has generated alternative interpretations and is said it could either represent the rebirth of Balder, son of Odin and the Viking god of light, or the crucifixion of Christ. Interestingly, there were two early Norse crosses at one time but the other was taken down, broken up and made into a sundial in the 1700s.

St Mary's Church originally dates from around 1100 but has been renovated several times, most recently in the late 19th century.

The cork tree, which was planted in 1833 is the most northerly example in Europe.

The toolshed in the corner of the graveyard is built of stones from the original church and is now a listed building.

Inside the church are two Viking Hogback stones, which were discovered in the foundations of the church's north wall during the last renovations in the late 1800s. These are known as the Saint's Stone, supposedly the grave cover of an early saint, and the Warrior's Stone, which is thought to have covered the grave of a Viking warrior.

The graveyard contains a cork tree, which was planted in 1833 and is the most northerly example in Europe. *Quercus suber* is a type of oak tree which is native to the Mediterranean region. The tree has adapted to problems of fire and drought by growing thicker bark as a protective layer. This cork layer has many industrial uses and huge open forests have been

St Mary's Church originally dates from around 1100 but has been renovated several times, most recently in the late 19th century.

developed to benefit from its sale in seven countries bordering the Mediterranean. Portugal is the world's largest producer, followed by Spain.

Cork oak trees are not felled, but at harvest time the bark is stripped by hand using a special axe. This layer slowly regenerates, creating a sustainable crop. Areas are harvested in rotation every nine to 12 years, often with little or no work carried out in between these times. This, of course, provides an important and safe habitat for wildlife. A tree will be approximately 50 years old before its bark will be suitable for a wine stopper and may live to be from 200 to 400 years old.

The toolshed standing in the corner of the graveyard beside a small gate is built of stones from the original church and is now a listed building. Some historians believe its original use may have been as a shelter for the watch committee, which was formed during the 17th and early 18th centuries after a grim profession emerged. A growing number of anatomists, keen to improve their medical knowledge, needed corpses on which to conduct dissections, which were often done in 'theatres', where members of the public could pay to watch. Bodies were difficult to come by because it was only legal to perform a dissection on the corpse of a recently executed criminal. So 'body snatchers', also known as 'resurrection men', made money by digging up fresh corpses and selling them to medical schools and hospitals.

Poor graves were easiest to plunder, as paupers were often buried in mass graves that were left uncovered for a few weeks, until they were full of coffins. Single graves were trickier and the body snatchers' preferred method was to dig a narrow hole down to the coffin, break through the wood and pull the body out attached to a rope. Corpses were then transported in sacks and barrels, often disguised as merchandise. A body was not considered anyone's property and so could be taken, but taking the shroud it was wrapped in was considered theft, so that was left behind.

People were so afraid of being torn from their graves that the rich paid for metal coffins, or wooden caskets bound in metal bands called 'mort safes' and some churches even constructed buildings to house groups of men to keep watch over the recently buried. It is believed the shed at St Mary's is an example.

Grange-over-Sands

Grange-over-Sands is a quiet seaside retreat on the Southern tip of the Cartmel peninsula, between the mountains and the sea on the shores of Morecambe Bay. From the 13th century until the 1850s the major route from Lancaster was across the sands. In 1887, the coming of the Furness Railway encouraged the growth of Grange from a small hamlet to a prosperous small town. Wealthy industrialists from Lancashire and Yorkshire were quick to build large houses here, taking advantage of the more convenient access. The Ulverstone and Lancaster Railway first opened on 28 August 1857 and the first passenger train ran on 1

In 1887, the coming of the Furness Railway encouraged the growth of Grange from a small hamlet to a prosperous small town.

September. The Furness Railway took over the UandLR in 1862 and commissioned respected architect Edward Paley of Lancaster to design the new station at Grange-over-Sands, which was built between 1864 and 1872. It is believed to be a replica of the top storey of the Grange Hotel, which is situated opposite.

The Victorian promenade is the place to enjoy the bracing sea air.

Sarah Nelson's gingerbread shop can be found in the corner of St Oswald's churchyard.

Sarah Nelson's Gingerbread Shop

Just north of Lake Windermere is the village of Grasmere, once the home of Lakeland poet William Wordsworth and also the home of Sarah Nelson's gingerbread shop. This little shop can be found in the corner of St Oswald's churchyard. It was originally the village school and dates from 1630. It has changed little over the years, in fact the school coat pegs are still there and so is the little cupboard where the school slates were kept.

Sarah Nelson was born Sarah Kemp in the little lakeside town of Bowness-on-Windermere in 1815, the year the Battle of Waterloo was fought. As a child she suffered a hard life of poverty; her poor widowed mother was only too pleased to be able to get her into service with the local gentry. But Sarah worked hard and her sober diligence saw her eventually work her way up to the position of cook. In 1844 she

The shop was originally the village school.

married Wilfred Nelson from Morland near Penrith, but marriage did not make life any easier. Wilfred earned his living as a farm labourer and supplemented his meagre income by also working as a part-time grave digger, but even so he could still not bring in enough money to support his wife and their two children, and so Sarah had to take in washing and make cakes and pastries for Lady Farquhar of Dale Lodge in Grasmere to help make ends meet.

In about 1850, Gate Cottage at the corner of the churchyard came up for rent. This tiny cottage had been built by public subscription as the village school. Education was not compulsory at this time, and it was only the more well-off folk in the village who could afford the penny a day to send their boys to school. In the second half of the 19th century, of course, education became compulsory and a new school had to be built to accommodate all the village children, allowing Sarah and her family to move in to the little property. Lady Farquhar's French chef taught Sarah to make gingerbread and she sat out in her little cobbled

yard selling her homemade gingerbread, cakes and drinks to the Victorian tourists who came to Grasmere. Her gingerbread became so well-known and in such great demand that she took the precaution of locking her recipe away in the local bank vault. Sarah died in 1904 at the age of 88 but fortunately her secret lived on, as her secret recipe passed to her great niece who sold it on to Daisy Hotson, who went into partnership with Jack and Mary Wilson, whose nephew runs the business today.

Great Salkeld

The village of Great Salkeld lies deep in the lovely Eden Valley, has a population of some 400 people and is centered round the village pub and the Norman church of St Cuthbert.

There has been a church in the village since AD 880, when the body of St Cuthbert is said to have rested here during its epic journey from Holy Island to Durham. The church was extensively rebuilt in 1080 – the pillars and capitals are beautifully carved with figures of

beasts, birds and serpents, a reminder of its Norman heritage. The distinctive pele tower was added in 1380 with an iron door or yett to protect the people of the village from any incursions by Scottish reivers. The entrance to the tower is only 2ft 7in wide, another feature of a fortified church, and it also has a fireplace which would keep the villagers warm during sieges and a dungeon in the basement for any captured enemy raiders. This building is regarded, along with Newton Arlosh and Burgh-by-Sands, as one of the finest examples of a fortified church erected in the border area during the 14th century.

Before the coming of the railways the village was the point where several droving routes converged – it was a well-known and popular stop on the cattle drives to the south. The village pub, the Highland Drove, serves as a reminder of those days and was once the stopping place for the drovers, whose animals were watered at the Dub just outside the village, now home to rare Great Crested Newts.

The village was the birthplace of the Lord Chief Justice of England, Edward Law

St Cuthbert's Church is regarded as one of the finest examples of a fortified church erected in the border area during the 14th century.

The Dub just outside the village was once used by drovers as a watering hole for cattle but is now home to rare Great Crested Newts.

arrested be brought before a court for formal charge. If the charge is considered to be valid, the person must submit to trial; if not, the person goes free. When the law is suspended, then individuals can be imprisoned indefinitely and without charge. He was also a great advocate of the full range of corporal and capital punishment – especially the pillory – and it was he who sentenced Lord Cochrane to an hour in the pillory for defrauding the stock exchange in 1814.

He is not remembered with affection.

Greystoke – St Andrew's Church

The name Greystoke is thought to have derived from an Anglo-Saxon word, *Creikstak* which translates as 'the place by the meandering stream'. The foundation of the church of St Andrew dates back to the mid-1200s. It was probably dedicated to St Andrew by the monks

(1750–1818). It was Edward Law who defended the suspension of *Habeas Corpus* – a legal writ that protects an individual against arbitrary imprisonment by requiring that any person

The Highland Drove Inn serves as a reminder of the days when the village was a well-known and popular stop on the cattle drives to the south.

of Hexham Abbey who established a number of churches dedicated to him in the area. The Scots had already claimed Andrew as their patron Saint prior to the Norman Conquest and Cumbria lay within the Scottish province of Strathclyde at that time. Greystoke Church was first mentioned in historical records in 1255 when the rector, Thomas de Veteripont, was consecrated as Bishop of Carlisle. At that time the church was richly endowed by the 10th Baron of Greystoke and was second only to Carlisle Cathedral in that respect.

In those days the nobility took a keen interest in their parish church and it was the 14th Baron Greystoke, William, who provided the finance to enlarge the church to incorporate six chantries into its fabric where masses could be said. The walls of the central arcade were opened up allowing three chantries to be incorporated on each side, and each of these small chapels would have been enclosed by beautifully painted oak screens. As well as the six priests who presided over the chantries, another eight priests were appointed in the 14th century – this was in response to the devastating plague of the Black Death in 1348 in which more than half of the clergy in England died, leaving many parishes without a minister. These 14 priests lived together in a nearby college. They followed a way of life based on monastic

The great east window is a splendid collection of mediaeval glass.

Father Forgive, the striking sculpture on the west wall by Josephine de Vascanellos.

The college memorial with the alabaster effigies of William, the 14th Baron, and his grandson John, the 16th Baron.

traditions, but perhaps a little less strict, and would go out into the surrounding area in pairs, teaching and spreading the word of their religion. The college would also have had a master of grammar who would teach the boys of the parish – it was from these collegiate churches that our grammar schools and places like Eton, Winchester, Oxford and Cambridge evolved.

However, during the Reformation the college of Greystoke was closed and the chantries were outlawed. Sadly, the beautifully decorated screens were removed but left a very large nave.

There was an attempt to re-establish the college in 1958 but this time as a pre-theological college for the benefit of men with little or no

The church has some excellent examples of beautifully carved misericords.

academic background to prepare themselves for full residential training. They were lodged with local families and in addition to their studies they did practical work to support themselves. All 90 men who started this new college are now ordained in the Church of England but sadly the scheme closed in 1979 because of a lack of candidates.

The chancel recess is now dedicated as the college memorial containing the alabaster effigies of William, the 14th Baron, and his grandson John, the 16th Baron. For over 250 years these effigies lay outside of the church and have consequently suffered badly from water erosion – not to mention pieces that have been broken off by farmers to rub on sheep scab – a traditional cure – or to sharpen scythes!

The sculpture of the crucified Christ on the west wall is by Josephine de Vascanellos and is called *Father Forgive*, representing the words of Jesus to the good thief, crucified beside him, 'Today shalt thou be with me in paradise'.

Josephine de Vascanellos, a Londoner, was born to an English Quaker mother and an atheist Brazilian diplomat father. Her artistic pursuits were always supported by her parents, but her governess was forbidden to even mention religion. In 1921 she gained a scholarship to the Royal Academy and by the age of 19 she was accepted to the Grand Chaumiere in Paris where she studied under Bourdelle, one of Rodin's assistants. In 1930 she was drawn to the artist Delmar Banner, who was also an Anglican lay priest and whom she later married. He led her to be baptised into the Anglican church, a faith that has run through much of her artistic work. They adopted two boys, and the family settled in a farmhouse at The Bield in Little Langdale at the heart of the Lakes. She died in July 2005 at the age of 100 and was renowned as a gifted musician, composer, poet, dancer and inventor.

The great east window at St Andrew's is a splendid collection of medieval glass. The story is that the glass was removed as Cromwell's army approached and hastily buried. It was restored in 1848, but the restorers had difficulty in putting all the pieces back in the right places!

Greystoke Church is a wonderfully peaceful and spiritual place – an absolute treasure trove of interest and discovery – not to mention the absolute thrill of the red squirrels that can sometimes be seen in the churchyard.

Hardknott Roman Fort

Hardknott Roman Fort, or Mediobocdum as they called it, is sited on a remote three-acre plateau in a commanding a strategic position just below the famous Hardknott Pass. The fort was built between AD 120 and AD 138, during the reign of the Emperor Hadrian; however, it was abandoned during the mid-second century and then reoccupied in AD 200. Some historians believe that the Romans continued to use it until well into fourth century.

The fort must have been one of the loneliest outposts of the Roman Empire and would have been garrisoned by about 500 infantry troops – the Fourth Cohort of Dalmations. The clearly marked remains include the headquarters building, commandant's house and bath-house. The site of the parade-ground – the best preserved in England – survives beside the fort, and the road which Hardknott guarded can be traced for some distance as an earthwork. This road extended from Glannoventa Fort at Ravenglass and along the Eskdale Valley before continuing over the high, wild, rugged Hardknott and Wrynose Passes to Galava Fort on the eastern side of the mountains at Ambleside. Hardknott was an important military site for the Romans, a vital link in the chain of connecting forts and roads that ensured military control of the local tribes in the area.

The entrance to the fort was through the *Porta Praetoria* or main gate, which is sited to the south-east. The *Via Praetoria*, or main road,

Hardknott Roman Fort from the summit of Harknott Pass.

Hardknott Fort must have been one of the loneliest outposts of the Roman Empire.

led straight through this to the main headquarters building. The gate would have had double portals, which may have supported a gatehouse above the gates which would have been served by the wall walk. The most important building in the fort was the headquarters building, or *Principia*, which was in a central position at the junction of the two main roads entering the fort. The *Praetorium*, or commanding officer's house, seemed to have been a quite large, single-storied building and probably had its rooms built around a central courtyard. The rank and file soldiers would have been housed in wooden barracks. The fort had two granaries, or *Horrea*, to store the grain

which was the main part of the soldiers' diet. The wooden floor of the granaries would have been suported on rows of piers, rather like a hypocaust, to allow ventilation, and the bases of these piers are still visible.

The bath-house stands just outside the fort's walls, and the remains show that there were three adjoining rooms, the *Frigidarium*, or cold room, *Tepidarium*, or warm room and *Caldarium*, the hot room. There was another building situated nearby, this was circular in shape and known as the *Lacoricum* – a type of sauna. Two furnaces situated close to the *Caldarium* would have provided hot water for the baths.

Hardknott is regarded as the best preserved Roman Fort in Cumbria, and although it is exposed to the elements, it affords wonderful breathtaking views across the Lakeland fells as far as the distant Irish Sea.

Sited in this lonely elevation at the top of Hardknott Pass on the road over the mountains, it is still considered relatively isolated and difficult to approach even in modern times.

The bath-house of Hardknott Roman Fort, looking back towards the pass.

The granaries at Hardknott Roman Fort.

Hawkshead Old Grammar School

The Old Grammar School was founded in 1585 by the Archbishop of York, Edwin Sandys. The ground-floor classroom still has many of the old desks covered in carving done by the boys, including the poet William Wordsworth and his brother John. For over 300 years the school provided a classical education for boys between the ages of eight and 17 years old. Its reputation was excellent and it was regarded as one of the best schools in England – and the University of Cambridge is recorded as saying it 'produced the finest mathematics students'. As well as being the village school it also catered for

The Old Grammar School in Hawkshead was founded in 1585 by the Archbishop of York, Edwin Sandys.

boarders; and although there was no charge for education, board and lodgings had to be paid for, consequently most of the pupils came from wealthier families. However, some of the poorer boys were still able to attend by getting support from charitable funds.

The main schoolroom has many of the original desks used by both masters and pupils – the oldest, arranged against the walls, date from 1675 while the others are Victorian. Quite a few of the desks are carved with the initials and names of former pupils. This seems to have been tolerated, although would possibly have been difficult to stop because all the boys carried pen knives which were used to sharpen their quills. The most famous piece of graffiti is where the young William Wordsworth carved his name – now carefully preserved under perspex.

The pupils would learn Greek, Latin and mathematics and up to 70 boys, in three or four classes, would be taught in this main room each under either a master (the head), an usher (teacher) or an assistant (pupil-teacher). The competing activities must have made for an interesting exercise in concentration! The boys worked from six in the morning until 11am and then from 1pm until 5pm in the evening during

William Wordsworth's carved signature is carefully framed and preserved under perspex.

Carved graffiti on almost every wooden surface seems to have been tolerated, or maybe unavoidable, because all the boys carried pen knives which were used to sharpen their quills.

the summer and two hours less in the winter. They enjoyed three weeks' holiday at Easter and another three weeks at Christmas.

In Wordsworth's day the boys would pay an annual fee of one guinea plus additional charges for some subjects and also the tradition of paying a 'cockpenny' to the headmaster to allow them to bring birds to school for cockfighting. The boys lodged in houses around the village and William lodged with Ann Tyson and her husband who were in their 60s. He paid 12 guineas a year plus extra for candles, coal, tea and sugar.

The school closed in 1909.

Hawkshead

Hawkshead is an ancient township that was established in Norse times. It takes its name from Haukr, a Viking lord who first settled here. However, it is still the same tiny village of quaint houses, curving archways and intimate squares much loved by William Wordsworth and

Beatrix Potter. It belonged to Furness Abbey until the 12th century and the monks owned the nearby mediaeval manorial farm, Hawkshead Hall, right up to the Dissolution of the Monasteries in 1537. After this Hawkshead gradually grew and prospered – it was sited at the junction of the old packhorse routes linking the ferries of Windermere with the Coniston valley, and was a natural place to hold a market. It was James I who granted its Charter in 1608. All the usual goods were sold along with hardwood, charcoal and wool – spinning was a busy and prosperous trade that developed from this. In an attempt to stimulate even more growth in the wool industry, an Act of Parliament was passed – the 'burial in wool' certificate – which ordered woollen shrouds be used for the dead.

At one time the market was so busy that the village supported seven inns, although this has now been reduced to four. Overlooking the village square is the Market House which is where butchers used to sell their wares. At one time a stream flowed down the middle of Flag Street and provided water for the villagers, but it is now covered over with flagstones. The streets still have names connected with the businesses that once traded there – for example Leather, Rag and Putty Street is where tailors, glaziers and cobblers all plied their trades.

On a small hill overlooking the village is the church of St Michael and All Angels. It was first mentioned as 'the capella de Hawkeset' shortly after 1200 when its revenues were transferred to the Abbot of Furness. There are no remains from that time to be seen, although Nikolaus Pevsner suggests the jambs of the north doorway date from the 13th century, and it is possible that some of the walling is from the 14th century. But most of the building is 16th and 17th century in date, with added improvements incorporated in subsequent years. Up until 1875 the church was roughly rendered and painted white. Wordsworth refers

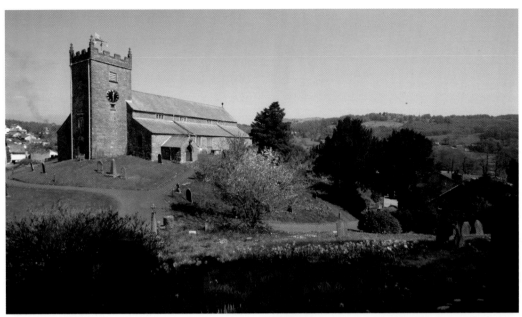

The church of St Michael and All Angels overlooks the village from a small hill.

Hawkshead is a beautiful little village of small whitewashed cottages and a maze of secret cobbled alleyways.

The streets have names connected with the businesses that once traded there.

WORDSWORTH STREET
FORMERLY LEATHER. RAG & PUTTY STREET

to this in his autobiographical work *The Prelude* when he came back to Hawkshead in 1788 after his first year at Cambridge:

I saw the snow-white church upon her hill
Sit like a throned lady sending out
A gracious look all over her domain.

Wordsworth was educated at Hawkshead and indeed found much inspiration here for his early poetry. From 1779 to 1787, he went to the Old Grammar School founded in 1585 by Dr Edwin Sandys.

Among its many its many literary connections are those with Beatrix Potter, who married the local solicitor, William Heelis, in 1913. What was his office is now the Beatrix Potter gallery and houses an annually changing exhibition of a selection of her original drawings and illustrations. She too found inspiration in Hawkshead and, interestingly, the character Johnny Town-mouse was based on the village doctor, Dr Parsons, who was a great friend of her husband.

Hawkshead is a beautiful little village of small whitewashed cottages and a maze of secret cobbled alleyways that run through overhanging arches, which has succeeded in preserving its quaint tranquillity over the years.

Herdwick Sheep

Lambing usually takes place between the middle of April and the middle of May.

Herdwick sheep are the native breed of the central and western Lake District and are well adapted to live on the highest of England's mountains. They are extremely hardy and are managed in the traditional way on the Lake District fells that have been their home for generations. Romantic tales that these tough grey sheep came from shipwrecked galleons from the Spanish Armada may or may not be true. But certainly the word Herdwick means 'sheep pasture' and can be traced back to the 12th century. They were originally kept for their wool, which was one of the main sources of England's early wealth, and this is where tradition of the Woolsack – the seat of the Lord Speaker in the House of Lords – is derived. Its history dates back to the reign of Edward III when the wool trade was one of the most important parts of the economy. A seat stuffed with wool was therefore a very important symbol of the wealth of the country.

Herdwick fleeces keep out the worst of weathers, the sheep can survive on very little vegetation and are said to be the only pure breed of sheep able to live on the high Lake District fells throughout the year. They are also

An inquisitive Herdwick ewe.

suited to life on the open fells because they have an inbuilt heafing instinct. This means that stay on or close to their own part of the fell. When flocks do get mixed up, farmers are able to recognise their own sheep by means of special sheep 'marks'. Each sheep is marked in two ways: with a 'lug' mark where part of the ear is clipped out, and a 'smit' mark, made with a chemical dye on the fleece. These marks for each individual flock are recorded in the *Shepherds' Guide.*

The sheep are rounded up and brought down from the fell four or five times during the year, for dipping or spraying, dosing, shearing, tupping and lambing. Before compulsory dipping was introduced in 1905, the sheep were just washed in handy deep pools. They were herded into the wash-fold on the beck (stream) edge and thrown into the water where they were dunked and then allowed to swim to the other bank. However, chemical dipping in a tub made sure that the wool was thoroughly washed and the sheep were protected from blowfly and scab. Today many farmers prefer spraying rather than dipping their animals.

Shearing or clipping takes place at the beginning of July, when the whole flock is

Herdwick lambs.

driven down from the fell to the farm. Today, most farmers use electric shears to shear off the wool, but there are a few who still like to use the traditional hand-shears. When clipping by hand, farmers would sit astride a slatted stool or creel with the sheep upended in front of them and hold the sheep steady with one hand while clipping with the other. Before the widespread use of electric shears, making the job much quicker, hand-shearing was a communal and indeed social occasion, with each farmer helping his neighbours. After being shorn, the sheep are smitted or marked before being returned to the fell.

In November, the tups or rams are put to the ewes. Traditionally, tups were hired at the Autumn Tup Fairs, kept for the winter and then returned in May; although today most farmers have their own tups. Herdwicks are smaller than the average sheep, and a ewe can die or become physically weak and stunted if she has lambs when too young. A 'Twinter' is a sheep approaching her second birthday and a 'Thrinter' her third. Some 'Twinters' are bratted or clouted, whereby a piece of clout or a 'brat' is sewn over their rear ends as a simple but effective form of contraception. A 'brat' is local dialect for a stout apron made of coarse, heavy-duty cloth or clout. This brat would remain in place from mid-November until February. These sheep would then lamb as 'Thrinters'. The mature sheep are then taken back to the fell for the winter months. Hay, baled silage, concentrates and mineral blocks are put out to supplement their diet. The young sheep or 'Hoggs' (lambs in their first year) are often wintered in more sheltered places, such as around the farm, near the coast or on lowland farms which will aid their growth and survival. In March the sheep are herded down to the intakes and pastures for a few weeks before lambing, which usually takes place between the middle of April and the middle of May. At the end of May the ewes and lambs are returned to the fells until July when shearing takes place.

Herdwicks are slow-growing sheep with a low lambing average compared with lowland breeds. This and their free-ranging grazing gives the meat a unique quality and stronger flavour. These days the commercial value of wool is negligible even though it is tough and wiry and creates garments which are exceptionally warm and that can repel rain and outlast many softer fabrics – a great recommendation is that this is what John Peel's 'Coat so Grey' was made from! And so it is the excellence of the Herdwick meat that is now the greatest value to the Cumbrian farmer.

Honister Slate Mine

Honister slate mine is situated at the very top of Honister Pass, which connects Buttermere with Borrowdale. Originally, in the 17th and 18th centuries the high-grade Honister slate was quarried, but by the middle of the 19th century underground mines were also in operation and in 1879 the Buttermere Green Slate Company was formed. This business closed down in 1986, but the mines were opened up again in 1997. The slate is now taken from underground tunnels only. Although other Lakeland slate comes in a variety of shades and colours, Honister slate is a distinctive green colour. It is a strong and long-lasting material, excellent for roofing and many other building purposes where durability is of utmost importance.

The mountains surrounding the mine all yielded up the hard green slate, which was formed from 400-million-year-old volcanic ash. In the early days the slate was brought out of the mines on sleds. After loading up a sled with up to 500lbs of slate, a worker would bravely pull it down the steep mountainside, running in front of the sled. If he lost his footing or was not quick enough, the sled could overrun and crush

him. Several loads a day were the normal punishing working routine. After dressing, the slate was carried to the coast at Ravenglass by trains of packhorses climbing up over the western edge of Great Gable and through Wasdale. In the latter half of the 19th century a tramway and aerial ropeway replaced the sleds to move the slate from the mines. Until a purpose-built slate finishing building was constructed in the 1920s, miners often finished the slate on site inside the mines or in stone huts built near the quarries. In the early days the

The climb up to the slate mines.

The entrance to the Kimberley mine, which is just one of the Honister slate mines.

A briefing is given to visitors before entry into the mine.

slateworkers lived at Honister during the week in small stone huts known as a bothys. By the 20th century an accommodation barracks had been built, just about where the modern youth hostel stands, and the company had also built a few houses in Borrowdale for its men.

The slate was extracted from the mine in large blocks known as 'clogs', and these had to be 'docked' or cut down by cutting across the

In the first cavern.

grain with a mallet and chisel. After the mid-1800s this method of working was replaced by sawing. The block would be further 'rived', or spilt down the grain, to produce thin slates which would be then further dressed on a slate anvil using a slate knife or 'whittle' to shape them uniformly. This process was also eventually mechanised, although many of these traditional skills are still practiced by today's mine workers in demonstrations for visitors.

Naturally, there are many stories of strange and notorious characters associated with the slate mines – one such character was Moses Rigg who, it is said, was a part-time smuggler along with his regular job at the mine. He would fill his empty pack with illegal spirits and other contraband on his way home from the mine. His customers for the produce of his illegal whisky included the landed gentry in addition to the local people. He was a popular target with the local Excise officers who competed to catch him; although this must have been frustrating for them because the most severe punishment he was ever given was a fine – probably because the magistrates were among his regular clients!

Underground guided tours of the mine are available, bringing to life the history and working of Honister, and for the more brave and adventurous there is the Via Ferrata – an adventure climbing system that uses a permanently fixed cable for safety and protection up the rock face of the old miners' route.

Many miles of mine tunnels run through the mountain.

Kendal

Kendal is a large market town situated on the River Kent, in the east of Cumbria, and is regarded the southern gateway to the Lake District. The town was built mostly from grey

Ladders and trackways network the mine tunnels.

Kendal's prosperity developed from the wool trade which started in the 13th century and flourished further in the 14th century with the arrival of Flemish weavers in the area.

limestone, and because of this it became known as 'the auld grey town'. Kendal was granted its Market Charter in 1189, and those days are remembered every spring with a mediaeval market with pageantry and music. Entertainment dominates the streets with strolling players, jugglers and jesters, while sellers ply their wares at market stalls.

Originally, Kendal's prosperity developed from the wool trade. It started in the 13th century and the trade flourished further in the 14th century when Flemish weavers arrived in the area. Right from this time until the 19th century, many mills were constructed on the River Kent to keep up with expanding production. The town's motto *Pannus Mihi Panis* – wool is my bread – relates to the famous 'Kendal Green', a rough, hardwearing material worn by Kendal archers. Memories of this important industry are recalled in many of the towns signs and street names, for instance, Tenterfell; the tenter was the frame on which wool was stretched and dried, held by hooks, hence the phrase 'on tenterhooks' meaning under tension.

The town's romantic old yards with cobbled lanes branch off and reconnect with the attractive main street. These yards were often named after the owners, and an excellent example is Yard 83, Dr Mannings's Yard, just off Highgate. The yards on this side of Highgate used to run in parallel lines down to the river, where there were factories, weaving shops, dying works and even a windmill. Yard 65 is called Windmill Yard. There were once about 150 'yards' in Kendal, and in the house at the top of yard 83 – originally called Braithwaite's Yard – George Braithwaite, a dyer, established a drysalter's business in 1713 supplying dyestuffs, alum, fuller's earth and other technical materials to the local textile trade. Further down the yard were workers' cottages, the counting house or office over the archway, a ropewalk, a weaving shed and a dyehouse. The Braithwaite family were well-known Quakers and philanthropists and set up a soup kitchen in the 'Hungry Forties' and a School of Industry for poor children.

DR MANNINGS YARD (83)

The town's romantic old yards with cobbled lanes were often named after the owners – an excellent example is Yard 83, Dr Mannings's Yard, just off Highgate.

Kendal has many treasures like this beautiful town house tucked away in its back streets.

The yard eventually became known by its present name of Dr Manning's Yard due to Dr Manning, who lived and practiced here for many years in the early 1900s.

Kendal is probably most famous for its Kendal mint cake. An amusing story tells how a Kendal confectioner, while trying to make glacier mints, forgot to keep a careful watch on the simmering candy and discovered that the mixture in the pan had turned cloudy and grainy. He poured it out anyway, and the rest is history – the world famous Kendal mint cake was born. This 'mistake' is credited to Joseph Wiper, who produced the cakes in his factory in 1869. His great nephew, Robert Wiper, supplied Kendal mint cakes as energy boosters to the 1914–17 Arctic Expedition under the command of Earnest Shackleton. Another company, Romney's, was founded by Sam Clarke, who owned a wholesale confectioners' business in Kendal, and in 1919 he bought an old mint cake recipe and established a factory. In 1953 this company supplied the high-energy Kendal mint cake to Sir Edmund Hillary's successful expedition to climb Mount Everest.

Kendal's more recent history has seen the rise, and fall, of industry, notably in snuff manufacture and shoe making. The noted and highly respected quality footwear manufacturers, K Shoes, was founded by the Somervell family in the 19th century and was

Kendal is well known for its 'yards', and at one time there were about 150 in the town.

The bristly hog on the wall outside Black Hall is a reminder that it was a brush factory in 1869, and in 1575 it was the home of Kendal's first Alderman, Henry Wilson.

Kendal – Sandes' Hospital

Sandes' Hospital in Highgate, across the road from the town hall, was built in 1659 and houses today, just as it always has, elderly persons. Just inside the gateway is an old iron collecting box engraved with the words 'Remember the Poore'. It was in this yard that Thomas Sandes, a cloth merchant and former Mayor of Kendal, who lived from 1606–1681, founded a school and eight almshouses for poor widows. The gatehouse was once the master's house and had single-story wings. It housed what came to be known as the Bluecoat School and a small library in the chamber over the gateway. The houses were rebuilt in 1852 by noted Kendal architect Miles Thompson. In 1886 the school merged with Kendal Grammar School which was succeeded in 1980 by Kirkbie Kendal School, whose trustees still own the property.

one of the town's main employers, but the company was taken over and the main manufacturing base moved elsewhere. Kendal was also the home of Alfred Wainwright MBE (17 January 1907 to 20 January 1991) the noted fell walker and author, whose *Pictorial Guides* have been in continuous publication since they were written and have sold more than two million copies. In 1930, at the age of 23, Wainwright first saw the Lakeland fells. This moment marked the start of his 'love affair with the Lake District'. In 1941 he was able to move closer to the fells when he took a job – and with it a pay cut – in the Borough Treasurers office in Kendal, Westmorland, as it was then. He lived and worked in the town for the rest of his life, and held the position of Borough Treasurer from 1948 until he retired in 1967.

Kendal has a long, chequered and proud history and its wonderful historic buildings, galleries and museums give depth and meaning to a visit to this friendly, bustling and charismatic Cumbrian town. It is an absolute treasure. Go there. Now.

Sandes' Hospital in Highgate was built in 1659 to provide housing for elderly widows.

Thomas Sandes, a former Mayor of Kendal, founded a school and eight almshouses for poor widows known as Sandes' Hospital.

It was here that 40 boys and 30 girls were clothed and educated until they reached 14 years of age, and also where eight poor widows were given separate apartments and gardens, and each was given an allowance of 4s 11d per week. In the words of Mr Thomas Sandes, their benefactor, the hospital was, 'for the use of eight poor widows, to exercise carding and spinning wool, and weaving of raw pieces of cloth for cottons called Kendal cottons; and for the use of a schoolmaster to read prayers to the said widows twice a day, and to teach poor children till prepared for the free school of Kendal or elsewhere'.

This wonderful building has retained its 17th-century charm and is well worth seeing – as is the Shakespeare, which was Kendal's first purpose-built theatre opened at the top of the yard behind the pub of the same name next door in 1829. It was designed by local architect John Richardson and the famous actor Edmund Kean appeared here in 1832, but increasing poverty in the town and pressure from Quakers, Presbyterians and Temperance groups forced it to close within five years. It continued to be used as a ballroom for many years and in 1994 it was converted to use as the New Life Community Church.

Just inside the gateway of the hospital is an old iron collecting box engraved with the words 'Remember the Poore'.

The gatehouse was once the Bluecoat School master's house and housed a small library in the chamber over the gateway.

The ruins of Kendal Castle date from the 12th century.

Kendal Castle

The ruins of Kendal Castle can be found on a hill on the western edge of the town. The castle was originally an earth and timber construction, built by the de Lancaster family, the barons of Kendal. It was rebuilt in stone in the late 12th century by Gilbert Fitz-Reinfred, who became the owner through marriage. The castle then had several owners, including the Crown, and it was Richard II who granted ownership of the castle to the Parr family of which Catherine Parr, Henry VIII's sixth wife whom he married in 1543, was the daughter.

The ruins of Kendal Castle overlook the town.

Some historians believe she was born in Kendal Castle. However, the Parrs were not a particularly wealthy or prominent family before their connection with the king and afterwards they only lived in the castle for a short period. When it was no longer associated with the Parrs, the castle stopped being of any interest and it is recorded that by 1572 it had fallen into a ruinous condition and suffered the fate of many such neglected buildings by providing an easy source of ready dressed stone for other building projects. It was 1813 before any work was carried out to prevent further deterioration but unfortunately a poor attempt at restoration has obliterated any clues there may have been to the original look of the building. However, despite the careless ransacking, it is fairly obvious that the building had a central gatehouse, with a large hall on the left and the private apartments and ladies' quarters on the right. Only a small part of the latter building remains, and unfortunately the gatehouse has long since fallen into the moat. The two vaulted chambers on the left-hand side of the entrance were probably kitchens,

The remains of the large hall at Kendal Castle.

with a fireplace and flue and an arched drain leading to the moat.

Kendal Castle is easily accessible by good paths and there are excellent views of the town to be enjoyed from Castle Hill. It was bought and designated for 'public enjoyment' by Kendal Corporation in 1897, to celebrate Queen Victoria's Diamond Jubilee.

Keswick Railway Footpath

This four-mile-long footpath was created by the Lake District National Park Authority after it had acquired a section of the Cockermouth, Keswick and Penrith Railway, which had been closed to traffic in 1972. The 18 miles of the route between Penrith and Keswick had 78 bridges and eight of these cross the River Greta over the railway's three-mile length between Threlkeld and Keswick.

A lot of the track was obliterated by improvements to the A66, but the section between Keswick and Threlkeld through the Greta Gorge remains largely untouched by any road construction work and has left a series of impressive bridges to provide the route for a

scenic footpath. The route is well maintained and most of it is level, apart from a short stretch that passes underneath the A66 viaduct where the line used to go through a tunnel. This easy trail through beautiful countryside blends many natural and man-made features into an excellent walk which offers something of interest for everyone.

The Cockermouth, Keswick and Penrith Railway was originally built as a mineral line between 1862 and 1864, and linked Workington in the west to Durham in the east, and at Penrith it connected to the direct railway route

Keswick Station has a magnificent Victorian wrought iron and glass canopy stretching the full length of the platform.

Keswick's impressive Victorian station.

through the Pennines over Stainmore pass from the Darlington area and to the West Coast Main Line from London to Glasgow. The contractors were Matthew Boulton and Son of Newcastle, who submitted the successful tender of £267,000, and the engineer was Thomas Bouch, a native Cumbrian from Thursby who had been educated in Carlisle. He is probably better remembered for one of his later engineering works – the ill-fated Tay Bridge, which collapsed during a gale resulting in the death of 75 passengers and the crew of a train. Bouch was heartbroken at the disaster and sadly died within the year.

The CK and PR, as the railway was affectionately known, opened to goods traffic

on 26 October 1864 and to passengers on 5 January 1865. It provided a vital link in the railway chain which connected the two great iron producing areas of West Cumberland and Durham. Really it was an almost unknown railway; it had no locomotives or rolling stock of its own, apart from a few ballast wagons. Two of the more well-known railway companies actually worked the line: the London and North Western, and, in the early days, the Stockton and Darlington Railway which was eventually taken over by the North Eastern. Furthermore, from 1889 onwards two directors from each company sat on the board of the Cockermouth, Keswick and Penrith Railway. The process of closing the line was started in the 1950s; at the time the accountants calculated that it was losing over £50,000 a year and British Rail lost no time in announcing the intended closure of the whole line from Penrith to Workington.

However, before the final step was taken, BR looked at the possibility of introducing a series of economies on the line and, as one possible solution, on 3 January 1955, Derby Lightweight diesel multiple-units were introduced to handle

The 18 miles of the route between Penrith and Keswick had 78 bridges and eight of these cross the River Greta over the railway's three-mile length between Threlkeld and Keswick.

The route between Keswick and Threlkeld through the Greta Gorge is well maintained and most of it is level.

the passenger services, and this immediately led to an increase in profits.

Some of the goods trains were still being hauled by the old Victorian ex-LNandWR locomotives, and others by the relatively lightweight and classic BR locomotives. Despite making economies in the working of the line, BR still insisted it was losing money and in the 1963 Beeching Report the closure of the line was recommended.

On 1 July 1964, all goods services were withdrawn, and within a year BR announced that the line would be closed completely in April 1966. This statement fuelled a huge protest by local people but despite a bitter struggle all passenger services west of Keswick Station were withdrawn in April 1966, this just left an 18-mile-long branch from Penrith to Keswick. But it was claimed that the line was still losing money and even more economies were introduced. All second tracks were removed and signalling was dismantled, and after 1 July 1968 all remaining stations became unstaffed halts and the line was then worked by one Diesel Multiple Unit. However, BR

maintained that the branch was still losing money, and in November 1971 it announced that all passenger services would be withdrawn from 6 March 1972.

Keswick Moot Hall

A Moot Hall was used for the keeping of assize, sessions and as a temporary gaol. It would also usually have a meeting room on the first floor with either provision for shops, lock-ups or public meeting places on the ground floor. The Moot Hall in Keswick Market Square was built in 1813 and has an unusual one-handed clock marked to tell time accurately to the quarter hour, there being four divisions between each of the hour numbers rather than five when a clock is calibrated for minutes. It now houses the Tourist Information Centre on the ground floor and a busy art gallery above.

In January 2003, while work was being carried out on the Keswick Town Centre Improvement Scheme, a well was uncovered beside the Moot Hall. The existence of the well

The Moot Hall, in Keswick Market Square, was built in 1813.

was previously unknown and there is no clear indication of when it was dug. It appears to go underneath the Moot Hall which dates from 1813, and this means the well could be at least 200 years old. It is nearly 6ft across and almost 30ft deep and seems to have been lined with stone from the river. The well has been capped while the work continues in the town centre, but it is hoped that it will be a way to eventually incorporate this interesting find into the new market place landscaping.

King Arthur's Round Table and Mayburgh Henge

The site has nothing whatever to do with the legendary king it is named after and predates him by about 2,500 years – it dates from between 2000 and 1000 BC. King Arthur's Round Table is thought to have been named in the 14th century when the Clifford family moved into nearby Brougham Castle. They

claimed Welsh royal ancestry, which in turn was firmly believed to be descended from the legendary King Arthur.

The monument is not far from Mayburgh Henge and lies at the confluence of the Eamont and Lowther rivers. Like Mayburgh it dates from the late Neolithic or Bronze Age. The earth bank and ditch measure 162ft in diameter. Unfortunately, it has been altered extensively by the construction of two nearby roads. In 1820 it was further desecrated by a local pub landlord who carted in loads of landfill to raise the centre and used it as site for a tea garden. No artifacts or stones were found in the centre but sketches of the site made in the 17th century suggest that there may have been large monoliths flanking the entrance, but unfortunately there is no longer any trace of these.

There is a theory that there is some connection between King Arthur's Round Table and Mayburgh Henge, which faces the Round Table and is clearly visible through the entrance of Mayburgh, and it is possible that they were in some way linked physically and spiritually in the minds of the prehistoric population – but there is no real evidence to back this up.

Mayburgh Henge is in a quiet location just a few hundred yards from King Arthur's Round Table. This large henge monument is possibly one of the most impressive in Cumbria. It consists of a huge circular bank enclosing a central area about an acre and a half in diameter. In the centre of the henge is a solitary standing stone almost 9ft high, although there is evidence to suggest that in the 18th century there were four standing stones in the centre and a further four at the entrance. The surrounding banks are about 12ft in height and built from large boulders.

No official excavation has been done at Mayburgh, so it is difficult to date with any accuracy, but the presence of Neolithic and Bronze axes found near the site indicate that it could date from the Neolithic or Bronze Age

and may well have been a meeting place for a large prehistoric community.

Sited between King Arthur's Round Table and Mayburgh Henge is the Eden Millennium Monument, a 50 ton block of granite from Shap quarry that was erected here and dedicated on 2 July 2000 by the Bishop of Penrith as a major part of the Eden Millennium Festival. The site was chosen because of its association with neighbouring Meyburgh Henge, the 4,000-year-old Bronze Age amphitheatre which, it is

believed, was the first great gathering place in the Eden Valley. The granite is 330 million years old, and the monument is intended to last thousands of years. In a trench round the base 2,000 small stones are buried – decorated mostly by the primary school children of Eden and placed there at the dedication service as birthday presents for Jesus' 2,000th birthday. The carved symbols on the monument represent the beginning and the end, and the past and the future.

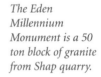

The Eden Millennium Monument is a 50 ton block of granite from Shap quarry.

Kirkbride

The village of Kirkbride is situated about five miles north of the town of Wigton. It has a history of involvement in Cumbria's traditional sports: wrestling and hound trailing. The Romans had a settlement here around the

The eerie Mayburgh Henge is difficult to date with any accuracy but there is evidence to suggest that it could date from the Neolithic or Bronze Age.

St Bride's Church, Kirkbride.

St Bride's Church, Kirkbride, showing the chancel from the nave.

second century AD and the scant remains of a fort can be found a few miles to the south of what was the later fort at Bowness-on-Solway. The fort at Kirkbride was possibly founded by Agricola and probably re-built during the second half of the Trajanic period as part of the Stanegate frontier. It is thought that the stone used to build many of the houses in the village came from Hadrian's Wall.

The little church dedicated to St Bride stands at the northern edge of the village of Kirkbride, overlooking the estuary of the River Wampool. It is thought that it stands on the site of an early Christian site, its name being first recorded in 1189. The church is mostly Norman, though the chancel arch is of Saxon origin, and the material used to build the church probably came from the nearby Roman camp – a ready supply of dressed stone. It is an excellent example of a 12th-century church, with a simple nave, chancel and bell-cote. The now blocked north door is known as 'The Devil's Door', as it was believed that evil spirits fled through here when a child was christened. In the chancel arch there is a wonderful 16th-century plaster cast of Jesus being carried to the tomb. The east window depicts the three Irish saints: St Patrick, St Columba and, of course, St Bride.

St Mary's Parish Church, Kirkby Lonsdale, was built between 1090 and 1130.

Kirkby Lonsdale

Kirkby Lonsdale is a historic market town situated in an Area of Outstanding Natural Beauty on the border of Cumbria, between the Lake District and the Yorkshire Dales. It is a very ancient settlement – Romans Saxons, Normans and Danes all left their mark here, and the town was included in the *Domesday Book* of 1086.

Many of the buildings are of grey stone and reflect a number of styles and periods, particularly from 17th and 18th centuries. The town is largely unspoiled with many traditional shops, flower-bedecked homes, narrow streets and secret yards. It was granted its Market Charter in 1227 from King Henry III. The markets were originally held in the churchyard and still take place on Thursdays in the market square. The parish church, built between 1090 and 1130, is dedicated to St Mary and still retains its Norman arcade and arched doorway, and both its south and north aisles run the full length of the church. The western tower has windows of 15th and 16th-century appearance but was somewhat rebuilt in the early 1700s.

Far left: The market cross in Kirkby Lonsdale.

Left: The gazebo in St Mary's Churchyard, Kirkby Lonsdale.

John Ruskin said, 'The Valley of the Lune at Kirkby Lonsdale is one of the loveliest scenes in England...and therefore in the world'.

Salt Pie Lane, where a crafty widow made salty pies to make her clients thirsty.

Far right: The old Swine Market Cross marks the place near the church where the little piggies went to market.

The grass in the churchyard is only cut once a year in order to encourage wild flowers and insects.

The grass in the churchyard is only cut once a year in order to encourage wild flowers and insects – this only adds to the quiet rural peace and ensures that in summer the grass is long and full of busy life and flowers. There are wonderful views from the churchyard to the north and the east and for that very reason an octagonal, four-arched gazebo was built in the late 18th or early 19th century. This view from the churchyard over the River Lune Valley is known as Ruskin's View because of a comment John Ruskin, the social critic, made after seeing the famous watercolourist J.M. Turner's painting of the scene. He said, 'The Valley of the Lune at Kirkby Lonsdale is one of the loveliest scenes in England...and therefore in the world'. Fittingly, The River Lune derives its name from the Old English word *Lon* which has its origins in an Irish Celtic word meaning 'health-giving'.

There is an interesting tale about the unusually named Salt Pie Lane, originally

known as 'Cattle Market Yard' because of the livestock sales held there. However, a cunning lady living in the yard made hot, salted mutton pies for sale to the traders. After eating the pies they had to go into nearby pub to slake their thirst, the landlord of which just happened to be a relation!

Kirkby Lonsdale has successfully retained its unique and special character. Despite great differences in the ages of the various buildings they have been blended into a pleasing and uniformly attractive town.

Kirkby Lonsdale – Devil's Bridge

The Devil's Bridge over the River Lune is a scheduled Ancient Monument dating from the 16th century and takes its name from a local tale about an old woman who outsmarted the Devil. This a legend that can be found all over Britain, but with minor variations from region to region. A distraught old woman was separated from her

The Devil's Bridge is a highly popular and traditional meeting place for motorcycle enthusiasts.

cow by the river and made a pact with the Devil. He agreed to build a bridge across the river, and his reward was the possession of the first soul to cross the bridge. The crafty widow then made her dog cross the bridge and ruined the Devil's plan to take her soul.

The Devil's Bridge at Kirkby Lonsdale.

Possibly the finest bacon sandwiches for miles.

The bridge is a highly popular and traditional meeting place for motorcycle enthusiasts, who flock here for what many of them believe to be the finest bacon sandwiches you can get!

Far right: A sacred spring flows under the nave and the cool, clear water is drawn from St Oswald's Well on the church's west wall.

Kirkoswald – St Oswald's Church

The village of Kirkoswald is situated eight miles to the north-east of Penrith. It was once a thriving market town and has some typical Georgian buildings, an original cobbled market place and a 17th-century inn, all mainly built from the local red sandstone. Its Market Charter was granted in the 13th century allowing an annual fair that was held on St Oswald's day, 15 August. The church, of course, takes its name from St Oswald, who was King of Northumbria in the seventh century, and who re-established Christianity in the north after the

St Oswald's Church has an unusual detached 19th-century stone bell tower.

*St Oswald's
Church,
Kirkoswald.*

Battle of Heavenfield in Northumberland in AD 634. He visited the area, after which the church was named in his honour. The present church, which is on the site of several previous buildings, dates from the 1800s. Unusually, a sacred spring lies under the nave and its well is on the church's west wall. On top of a grassy hill about 200 yards from the church stands the detached 19th-century stone bell tower – there is thought to have been a bell tower of some sort here on the summit since Norman times. This is not surprising, as a warning bell would have been needed because Kirkoswald was attacked by Scottish raiders several times in the 14th century; but the problems did not end there and over a period of many years the village suffered bad harvests and outbreaks of disease – the plague killed two thirds of the village population in 1598.

Lacy's Caves – Little Salkeld

Lt-Colonel Samuel Lacy lived in Salkeld Hall in the 1700s and once tried to blow up the stones at Long Meg Stone Circle to make milestones; however, a fierce storm blew up and his workmen fled in fear of their lives, convinced that the stones were conjuring up a punishment for the desecration of their circle!

Right: Looking out from the inside of Lt-Colonel Samuel Lacy's Caves.

Far right: The massive wooden porch beams still survive from when the chancel was built in 1523.

A precarious but exciting path leads to the enigmatic Lacy's Caves.

A pleasant walk along the River Eden from the charming village of Little Salkeld leads to Lacy's Caves. He is perhaps better known for this project on the banks of the Eden where five

Lacy's Caves – five rooms excavated from the soft sandstone about 25ft above the swirling River Eden.

rooms have been excavated from the soft sandstone about 25ft above the swirling river. Some historians believe that he used the caves as a wine store but more popularly it is thought that he entertained guests here in this small romantic labyrinth of rooms interconnected by arched doorways. And it has also been suggested that at one time he employed a resident hermit to add to the atmosphere.

Lanercost Priory, Brampton

King Henry II captured the area of Gilsland from the Scots in 1157 and appointed Hubert de Vaux as lord of the manor. The king encouraged the foundation of a new monastery in the area and it is traditionally accepted that Robert de Vaux, son of Hubert de Vaux, established the Augustinian Priory at Lanercost in 1164, in memory of his father.

The priory is sited in a tranquil, secluded, wooded spot in the attractive valley of the River Irthing, alongside the line of the ancient route from Newcastle to Carlisle.

Religious houses made attractive targets for marauding armies and Lanercost was given undivided attention by the Scots. In the years after the Battle of Bannockburn raids became more frequent and the monastery suffered several determined attacks during these years, two of which were particularly savage. One was led by the Earl of Buchan in 1296, and the other by William Wallace in 1297 during his violent rampage through the north of England.

Lanercost bears the distinction that it is the only English monastery that has been a royal residence – this was for almost six months when Edward I visited in 1306. He was on yet another military campaign against the Scots in spite of his age and poor health. He was so ill that he had to be carried on a litter. He was probably

Lanercost Old Bridge is a packhorse bridge that once carried the main Newcastle to Carlisle turnpike road.

suffering from the severe dysentery that would eventually take his life, and consequently his group made extremely slow progress on its journey to Carlisle, and Lanercost was where they called a halt on the laborious journey. The king was accompanied by Queen Margaret plus their numerous supporters and servants, probably over 200 people in all, and they all had to be accommodated at the priory. The chronicles record interesting details of his stay: the inner court alone included a personal bodyguard of seven Welsh soldiers, two

Robert de Vaux established the Augustinian Priory at Lanercost in 1164, in memory of his father.

Lanercost was given undivided attention by the Scottish raiders in the years after the Battle of Bannockburn.

Dacre Tower, which was built when Thomas Dacre, Deputy Warden of the English West March in 1552, converted part of the monastery to a private residence.

surgeons, a tent maker, an otter hunter, the keeper of the king's cows, the king's heralds, a furrier to catch rabbits and a man employed to catch birds with glue. A small herd of goats was also brought along because Edward believed their milk was beneficial to his health. One of the surgeons had a groom who was sent into Carlisle to buy herbs for the king's feet, and on 15 October four carts from Carlisle were hired to bring wax, almonds, rice, cloth, canvas and spices to Lanercost.

Edward believed pious conduct was a necessary help to military success and he had a whole arsenal of ornamented relics, including,

allegedly, an arm of St David, a nail from Christ's cross and even a saint's tooth, which he believed protected him against thunder and lightning.

The king had arrived at the end of September but was too ill to continue his journey until the following March, putting a severe strain on the finances of the monastery. The monks bitterly complained that they had been 'greatly impoverished' by his sojourn – there is a record that over 200 deer were killed during the stay of the Royal party. However, King Edward did not let the incapacity of his illness interfere with his dedicated persecution of the Scots because while he was at Lanercost the two captured brothers of Robert the Bruce were brought before him. He sent Thomas to Carlisle where he was to be dragged around the city by horses and then executed and his head displayed on a spike on the city gates; and Alexander was to have his head cut off immediately and also displayed on a spike on the city gates.

After the death of Edward I the Scots resumed their large-scale raids with enthusiasm, and in 1311 Robert the Bruce overran the priory and stayed for three days. Although there was only a small amount of structural damage, sacred vessels were damaged, treasure chests looted and religious artefacts wantonly destroyed. The unfortunate priors suffered this awful depredation while they were still recovering from the visit from Edward I.

The monks suffered another serious blow in 1346 when King David II and his army plundered the priory on his way to a resounding defeat at the Battle of Neville's Cross, near Durham. These raids on top of a widespread famine and rampant cattle disease in 1316 followed by the outbreak of the Black Death in 1349 must have caused the community serious difficulties. And, in 1386, the prior of Lanercost was captured by Scottish raiders and ransomed.

However, over the next century things gradually improved and the priory did recover.

Until the Dissolution of the Monasteries in 1536, that is, when on 4 March 1537 Henry VIII sent the Duke of Norfolk to close the priory; and although he did offer a temporary reprieve it was finally closed in January 1538.

The priory eventually came into the possession of Thomas Dacre, who fought at the Battle of Solway Moss and distinguished himself in the rank of Deputy Warden of the English West March in 1552. He converted part of the monastery to a private residence and created a garden, an orchard and a rabbit warren and built a dovecote in the grounds.

Lanercost eventually passed to the Howard family and in January 1929 was passed over into State Guardianship, and today it is in the care of English Heritage.

Little Salkeld Watermill

Little Salkeld Watermill is a small, 18th century corn mill which has been restored to full working order and is one of the country's few

working waterpowered corn mills still producing stoneground flour the traditional way. It was built in the second half of the 18th century from local red sandstone hewn from a small quarry not half a mile away.

At first it was just a two-up, two-down for the miller and his family and a one-storey mill with no granary. Local farmers would arrive by horse and cart with sacks of grain, wait for them to be milled, then head off home again. But the coming of the railways saw a dramatic change. The Settle to Carlisle line passed close by, and the Irish navvies brought in extra trade. Soon a millshop opened, and then the mill prospered and a granary floor was added, followed by two new overshot cast iron waterwheels to speed production. The miller then stored oats and roasted them, and made haver meal and porridge, and sent it south to Leeds and London and north to Glasgow and beyond. Eventually, because of the demand for lighter, cheaper bread, Thomas Carr built a huge steam-powered mill at Silloth and took away the business from Little Salkeld Mill and many similar little rural mills, and by the 1930s Little Salkeld Mill was a quiet little business again.

Lanercost Priory once played host to Edward I in 1157.

Little Salkeld Watermill is a small, 18th-century corn mill restored to full working order.

The flow of water is controlled by a mill-race which is in turn controlled by the opening and closing of the sluice gate.

However, an incredible growth in the demand for old-fashioned, naturally produced food full of quality ingredients has seen a great increase in business and the mill is regarded as one of the best and most well-known suppliers of bakery products in Cumbria.

The working of the mill has changed little since it was built – the flow of water is

When the waterwheel is fully turning it develops up to 10 horsepower.

controlled by a mill-race which is controlled by the opening and closing of a sluice gate at the weir just where the mill-race starts. When the sluice gate is open the water flows down to the mill at an average of a million gallons every day before rejoining the beck below the mill. The beck joins the River Eden half a mile downstream, which eventually flows into the Solway Firth north-west of Carlisle.

The miller opens the sluices that feed the wheel from inside the mill, using a series of pulleys. The sluice gates divert the water to run over the wheel. The water from the race runs down the mill chute and fills the buckets on the waterwheel. Eventually the weight of water in the buckets starts the wheel turning. It keeps turning until the water is diverted away from the wheel. The main wheel is 12ft in diameter, its buckets are 4ft 9in wide, and when the wheel is fully turning it develops up to 10 horsepower. When the buckets empty at the bottom of the wheel the water runs away under the millhouse and back into the beck.

As the wheel turns it drives a shaft that goes right through the wall into the mill. This shaft turns the 'pitwheel' which has bevelled teeth that rotates the power through 90 degrees and meshes with the 'crown wheel'. This also has bevelled cogs and drives the large upright oak 'mainshaft' – also on this is the 'spurwheel', whose cogs mesh with the stone nut which drives another shaft that drives the millstones directly. The millstones are made from French Burr stone, a very hard type of flint-like stone quarried near Paris.

The millstone at Little Salkeld was brought from France in sections in the late 19th century and then bound together with metal bands by a firm in Liverpool. They weigh over half a ton each. The lower of the two stones (the 'bedstone') is fixed in the floor. A spindle passes through it that connects with the upper stone (the 'runner') to drive it against the lower stone. The inside surfaces of the stones are dressed with a special pattern. These grind the grain and channel it from the centre (the 'eye') to the edges as milled flour. The grain takes a few seconds to pass from the eye as wholegrain to the edge of the stones ground to flour. Once ground and at the edge of the stones, the flour passes away down a chute to be bagged, sieved or blended.

Long Meg and Her Daughters, Little Salkeld

Along a very narrow lane on a hill about a mile from the village of Little Salkeld is the remarkable stone circle known as Long Meg and Her Daughters. It is said to be the largest such circle in England, with the exception of Stonehenge, and is also regarded as one of the most important archaeological sites in the country.

The circle is over 100 yards in diameter and is believed to date from around 1,500 BC, possibly the work of Bronze Age man. The circle is sited on working farmland, and in addition to the sheep grazing between the stones a public road runs right through the site. A local legend has it that nobody can count the stones – it is said a different answer is reached every time. Reference books suggest there are about 60 stones but no one seems to be able to make an accurate count and figures between 59 and 77 are mentioned (I got 64 – but maths has never been my best subject!). The legend of their magic powers is attributed to Michael Scott – the alleged wizard who is buried in Melrose Abbey. He is said to have endowed the stones with magical powers which means they can never be counted accurately. The stones are not of a uniform shape or type. There are granite, sandstone and limestone stones, some are almost level with the ground while others are taller than a person; some are relatively small and others are over 12ft in circumference – but they are all possessed of the magic power to stop anyone counting the same number twice!

Of all the stones, one in particular stands out – this is Long Meg. She is over 12ft tall and stands slightly apart from the others, but she does lean towards them at a slight angle. She stands alone but is 'watched' by four of her daughters who form a sort of gateway. Meg is said to have been a witch, a seductress or an

Meg is said to have been a witch, a seductress or an alluring dancing girl.

Long Meg and Her Daughters stone circle is over 100 yards in diameter and is believed to date from around 1,500 BC. It is possibly the work of Bronze Age man.

Little Meg is a smaller stone circle, about half a mile away but worth searching for, just out of curiosity.

alluring dancing girl – it would be rather nice to think she was all three! Another story says that she was named after a rather boisterous lady of the court of King Henry VIII.

Meg is engraved with ancient cup and ring markings – this form of decoration is quite common, such as at Roughtin' Linn in Northumberland – and was possibly produced through religious inspiration or, it has been suggested, is a small scale representation of stone circle geometry carrying astronomical information.

William Wordsworth travelled to see this site in 1821 and named the stones 'a family forlorn'. He said he had known of Long Meg since childhood but had never seen her until that moment – an impressive and unexpected sight. He estimated her to be over 18ft in height and declared her to be our most noble relic after Stonehenge.

About half a mile away, in the corner of a field, is a smaller stone circle, known as Little Meg, which only has 11 stones and is worth searching for out of curiosity even though it is only about 20ft across.

As to be expected, there are several sinister tales associated with Long Meg and Her Daughters. One of the most curious says that if a piece is broken off Meg she will bleed, and another tells that the surrounding stones were all her lovers who were turned to stone when they incurred her displeasure.

Another tale says that Meg and her daughters were a coven of witches who came here to perform their rituals. A local saint was outraged by their bawdy sacrilegious cavorting and uttered a powerful curse, which promptly turned them all to stone.

Another well-known tale concerns Lt-Colonel Lacy (of Lacy's Caves fame) when he decided to blow up the stones with dynamite. But as the preparations were being made a fearsome thunderstorm arose; the lightning was the most ferocious ever experienced in the area and the wrath of the storm made his workmen run for their lives and never to attempt to blast the stones – and there they remain.

Stone circles have always provided much material for speculation. They were dismissed as 'primitive' by the Romans and described as 'the Devil's work' by the early church. Such was the fear of these sites in the Middle Ages that the ecclesiastical authorities ordered the demolition of many of them – where they proved to be indestructible they had to be toppled and buried. Nowadays it is generally believed that stone circles were erected as places of assembly – sanctified by continuity for seasonal gatherings and the performance of rituals possibly associated with the elements or with the sun and moon.

Even so, these stones do seem to exert some deep kind of magic or mystery and are just as enigmatic as ever.

Arthuret Church on the outskirts of Longtown was originally founded about 1150 but was ruined in the cross-border conflicts of the 14th and 15th centuries.

Longtown

Longtown is a town of almost 3,000 inhabitants and is situated right on the border between England and Scotland, about six miles from Carlisle and about three miles from Gretna Green. It was planned and built in the 18th century by the Grahams of Netherby – descendents of that notorious border family.

The area has suffered a turbulent and unsettled but interesting history, no doubt fuelled by its position right on the edge of what was once declared the lawless 'Debatable Lands' in the days of Border Reiving.

Arthuret Church on the outskirts of Longtown was originally founded about 1150 but was ruined in the cross-border conflicts of the 14th and 15th centuries. The notorious reiver Richie Graham collected his 'blackmaile' protection money in the church porch – he also kept a list here of those who had paid, or perhaps, more to the point, those who had not paid and were due for a 'reminder'.

The church was extensively rebuilt in the early 1600s and dedicated to St Michael and All Angels. In the early days it was served by the monks of Jedburgh Abbey and its site is closely linked with the legend of King Arthur. The building was financed during the reign of King James I by raising a public subscription which organised on his order by the Archbishop of Canterbury, after the king had learned that his subjects had lost their faith and were without virtue or regard for religion. The building of the church presented King James with a great opportunity to make a significant gesture as part of his 'Pacification of the Borders'.

In 1746 Bonnie Prince Charlie's fleeing army crossed the River Esk at Longtown, hotly pursued by his cousin and sworn enemy, the Duke of Cumberland.

Arthuret Knowes is said to be where Urien of Reghed and his son Owain fought off an invasion of fierce Anglo-Saxon tribes in AD 573.

Near the unusual Maltese Cross in the churchyard is the grave of the charismatic Archie Armstrong who held the position of court jester and groom of the chambers to James I, and indeed to his son, Charles I. In spite of being the king's favourite it was Archie's inappropriate comment and badly received joke about Bishop Laude (during grace he cried 'All Praise to God and Little Laude to the De'il') that caused him to be relieved of his prestigious office and sent home to Longtown, forced into early retirement.

Not far from the church lies the battlefield of Solway Moss which was fought in 1542; James V had defeated the English at Haddon Rigg in August of the same year and his success encouraged him to press on with his army of, it is said, almost 18,000 troops to launch an invasion into England. He was met at Solway Moss by Sir Thomas Wharton with about 3,000 men. Wharton ordered his able deputy, William Musgrave, and his riders, or 'prickers', to harass

In Arthuret Churchyard is the grave of the charismatic Archie Armstrong, who was court jester and groom of the chambers to James I and his son, Charles I.

the enemy in a series of sporadic lightning attacks – it was the kind of work that well suited these able border riders. Their continued hitting and running, charging and retreating, eventually saw the Scots in disarray and confusion, and victory soon followed.

It was estimated that Wharton had only lost seven men while over 1,000 Scots were taken prisoner and many hundreds killed either by the English or in the dangerous bogs of Solway Moss. The Scottish army was routed and fled northwards, and they suffered the further indignity of being attacked and robbed on their way home and some arrived back in Scotland wearing only their hose and underpants.

In 1746 an army under the command of Bonnie Prince Charlie, the Young Pretender, Charles Edward Stuart, crossed the River Esk at Longtown, hotly pursued by his cousin and sworn enemy, the Duke of Cumberland. The river was almost in full spate and the Scots crossed by linking arms to affect a resistance to the powerful current. It is said that they were so relieved to make it safely back to the Scottish bank that they lit fires to dry themselves and celebrated their escape by dancing to the music of their regimental pipers.

The wooded hill across the fields to the east of the church is believed by some historians to be the site of the battle of Arthuret, fought in AD 573, when Urien of Reghed and his equally famous son Owain led an army made up of men from several tribes around the Solway to fight off an incursion of fierce Anglo-Saxon tribes from the east coast.

Lowther Castle and St Michael's Church

Lowther Castle has been the family seat of the Earls of Lonsdale for many centuries and occupies the site of mansions that date back to

the reign of Edward I. The present building was started in 1806, for Sir Hugh Lowther the fifth Earl, and was designed by Sir Robert Smirke – he was just 25 and this was his first job! It was commissioned to be a design of elegance, beauty and strength. The castle became well known for its wide range of activities and entertainment of distinguished guests. It was when the famous 'Yellow Earl', Hugh Lowther, lived there in the last decades of the 19th and first decades of the 20th century that the castle really became the centre of a social whirl: royalty, heads of state, politicians and all manner of the rich and famous of the time visited Lowther for parties and sporting weekends. The German Kaiser was a guest twice and brought the Earl a very early Mercedes Benz along with a German chauffeur! Hugh Lowther was a well-known motoring pioneer and many older people remember the sight of his fleet of yellow cars winding through the narrow roads near Askam.

The grounds were open to visitors in 1938 but were closed after being used to test secret tank weaponry during World War Two, though it has been suggested that during this more damage was done to Lowther than was done in Germany. Sadly, the castle's grand proportions were thought to be too extravagant for the 20th

century and after the death of the fifth Earl of Lonsdale the castle was abandoned, the interior was dismantled and only the walls left standing as a memorial to past glories.

The castle and its gardens have now been closed for 70 years and stand inaccessible and covered in vegetation. However, the Trustees of the Lowther Castle and Gardens Trust plan to transform the imposing remains of the Gothic castle, its massive stables and over 20 hidden gardens into a magnificent tourism, conference and visitor attraction.

St Michael's Church and its extensive churchyard are situated in Lowther Park not far from the romantic ruin of Lowther Castle. It enjoys a superb location overlooking the River

Lowther Castle has been the family seat of the Earls of Lonsdale for many centuries.

St Michael's Church dates from 1686 when the previous 13th-century church was rebuilt.

Lowther and there are fine views of forest and fell from the churchyard.

'Hogback' Saxon burial stones have been unearthed in the churchyard, and this would therefore suggest that this site has been used for Christian worship for about 1,000 years. The present building dates from 1686 when the previous 13th-century church was rebuilt – further improvements were carried out in the 18th and 19th centuries. In the churchyard, near the gateway, is the magnificent mausoleum of William, the second Earl, who died in 1844. Inside there is a statue of him sitting quietly in the all-enveloping silence.

Inside the church there are memorials to various members of the Lowther family. Behind the organ is a fine statue of Sir John Lowther who died in 1700, reclining life size, contemplating the coronet he holds in his hand. There are also magnificent busts of his grandfather and great-grandfather.

Maryport

Maryport is the southernmost town on the Solway Firth and for over 2,000 years has enjoyed a close association with shipping and the sea. However, in the early 1700s it was just a little fishing village at the mouth of the River Ellen consisting of no more than a few huts and a farmhouse. But by the end of the century, thanks to a local businessman called Humphrey Senhouse, who needed a good harbour for the export of coal from his estate, it was a thriving port of 20,000 people. In 1749 an Act of Parliament was passed to allow the creation of the present town which he subsequently renamed after his wife Mary – the name-change from Ellenport was approved by Parliament in 1791. Over the years various docks were added and the Senhouse Dock, the largest, was opened in 1884. At the near end of the South Pier is another rarity, the old iron lighthouse, which was built in 1846.

However, the origins of the town go back much further. The first major settlement was founded almost 2,000 years ago when the Romans arrived. They built a large fort on top of the 200ft-high cliffs to the north-east of the town and the remains of the gateways and defensive ditches are still visible. They called it Alauna and it was built as a command and supply base for the coastal defences of Hadrian's

The Elizabeth Dock in Maryport.

The Graving Bank, a sloped section of the quayside, made off-loading easier as cargoes could be easily winched ashore from rafts, boats and ships.

Wall at its western extremity. It was the last in a series of forts guarding the northern frontiers against attack from the Picts to the north and the Irish from across the sea. Recently, geo-magnetic surveys have established that there was a large Roman town surrounding the fort and there are plans to excavate the site in the near future. The first recorded occupant was a Roman officer called Marcus Maenius Agrippa, who was a personal friend of the Emperor Hadrian and at one time commanded a cohort of Spaniards.

There is evidence to suggest the fort was built around AD 122 but there was an earlier fort on the site, probably founded in Agricola's time in AD 79, which was then built over. The later fort was occupied for nearly 300 years until the army was recalled to defend Rome from the barbarians in AD 410.

There is very little known about what happened to Maryport after the Roman army departed but presumably, like most of the coastal area of Cumbria, it would have seen invasion and settlement by the Vikings. Evidence of their occupation can be found to

The Serpent Stone at Senhouse Roman Museum. This strange stone is worked into a phallic shape with a snake writhing its way up the shaft – this combines elements of Roman and Celtic symbolism offering protection from the Evil Eye.

*The Senhouse
Roman Army
Museum.*

the north of the town in Crosscanonby Church, which is an early mediaeval building and has a Viking hogback grave-cover and a Viking cross-shaft in the churchyard.

There is no mention of Maryport, or Ellenport as it was then known, in the *Doomsday Book*, just after the Norman Conquest in 1066, because the town and its surrounding area were then a part of Scotland. However, on a bend in the River Ellen, Motte Hill, a 12th-century motte and bailey castle, can be found, and this dates from the time when the area became part of England. It was subsequently abandoned in favour of Netherhall by the beginning of the 14th century. Eventually, in the 16th century, the manor of Alnburgh, as the area was known then, passed into the hands of the Senhouse family. And they were responsible for the development of Maryport and its harbour into the town we know today.

It was in the Victorian era that the town began to flourish; coal mines and an iron foundry contributed to its economic growth. The shipyards developed next to the docks and Maryport became famous for its ability to launch ships 'sideways' because of the narrowness of the River Ellen. It was also well-known for its Graving Bank – a sloped section of the quayside that made off-loading easier as cargoes could be easily winched ashore from rafts, boats and ships. The railway to Carlisle was built in the 1840s and George Stephenson was its chief engineer. Maryport thrived in these few good years and it was soon exporting huge quantities of coal.

Unfortunately, the town went into decline at the beginning of the 20th century and during the Depression in the 1930s adult unemployment peaked at a staggering 50 per cent.

There was a brief recovery during World War Two but inevitably in the succeeding years many of the mines closed, and the final open-cast site closed in 2000.

Today, on a more cheerful note, the town is looking a lot more confident with an exciting series of major regeneration projects enthusiastically underway.

Matterdale Church

Matterdale Church dates from the reign of Queen Elizabeth I, and, as was common with many old chapelries, has no formal dedication. However, these places of worship were deemed to have been hallowed by 'the reading of the Word and the prayers of the faithful'. The deed of consecration of the church dates from 1573, but the earliest certain date for the building is an inscription from 1686. The church was built as a chapel of ease for those living nearby in the tiny village of Dockray to the north-west of Ullswater, which, at that time, was within the Parish of Greystoke. It was here that a college of clergy was founded by Lord William of Greystoke and his heirs and licensed by the Pope in 1382 to serve the people of Greystoke, Watermillock, Matterdale, Mungrisdale and Threlkeld, but this was dissolved in 1548.

Matterdale Church dates from the reign of Queen Elizabeth I, and, as was common with many old chapelries, has no formal dedication.

The roof beam at the eastern end of the church has a curious inscription, with some initials and the date 1573. This date is taken to be the completion of the church, although there is a plaque showing the date 1686 and the initials G.S. – thought to be those of the mason.

From the outside the church is a simple structure with the nave and chancel in one – it has a sturdy, attractive south porch and a west tower of local slate which dates from 1848. There are two fonts, the older of which was in use from the 17th century until 1881, when a larger one from Greystoke was brought into use. The older one is now turned upside down and used as a sundial. The altar rails date from the late 17th century and were installed to keep animals from the altar. The main Christian festivals here are celebrated by candlelight.

Far right: Matterdale Church.

Right: The roof beam at the eastern end of the church has an inscription, with some initials and the date 1573. This date is thought to mark the completion of the church; although there is a plaque showing the date 1686 and the initials G.S. – thought to be those of the mason? Curious…

The village green was traditionally the main social space within a village.

The church can be found on the A5091 to the south-west of Penrith and is an excellent example of a small fell country church in a relatively remote yet easily accessible location and offers superb views over the surrounding countryside to the fells above Ullswater from the small churchyard.

Milburn, near Temple Sowerby

The village of Milburn, whose name derives from 'hill stream', is situated about three miles to the north of Temple Sowerby. It was originally held by Wetheral Priory during the reign of King John but it was it transferred to the de Stuteville family, then to the de Veteriponts and eventually came into the ownership of the Cliffords.

It is an excellent example of a mediaeval fortified village; its houses are arranged around a rectangular green covering just under five acres. The green was originally only open at its four corners, making it easily defendable as these entrances could be walled up in times of danger. This, of course, could also be convenient for penning livestock in winter. It was then that access was gained to the village through narrow and easily defended gaps between the houses.

The village green was the main social space within a village, as well as its focal point alongside the church, chapel or school. Village greens often take a triangular form, and reflect the fact that the village was at the meeting point of three roads. The continuing importance of the village green to modern day communities is reflected in that this is usually where the war memorial is seen, as well as village notice boards, where local cricket matches are played, and where public benches are placed.

Milburn is an excellent example of a mediaeval fortified village; its houses are arranged around a rectangular green covering just under five acres.

Access was gained to the village through narrow and easily defended gaps between the houses during times of trouble.

The Open Spaces Society records that there were about 3,650 registered greens in England and about 220 in Wales at the beginning of the 21st century.

The area is quite well known for its strong easterly wind, called a *helm*. Air rises on the Pennine slopes and as it moves up is rapidly cooled, and the helm forms near the summit of Cross Fell and then rushes down the western slopes. It is the effect of alternating currents of warm and cool air produce the strong winds that blow across the village.

Monk's Bridge

Monk's Bridge on Cold Fell is the oldest packhorse bridge in Cumbria and crosses Friar Gill where it passes through a deep narrow

chasm. These were traditionally high-humped, narrow, cobbled bridges often located in upland areas where most of the goods were carried by horses or ponies. It is thought that Monk's Bridge was built for the monks of Calder Abbey, who would probably have crossed it on their many journeys, and, of course, iron ore would have also been carried over it from Ennerdale to smithies on the fells to be smelted. The bridge is also known as Matty Benn's Bridge, after a family called Benn who lived nearby. These ancient trackways, some dating back to pre-history, have been used for centuries to transport goods across the land. Traders from overseas, monks, drovers, soldiers and pack

Milburn primary school dates from 1851.

Monk's Bridge is the oldest packhorse bridge in Cumbria and carries an ancient route across Friar Gill where it passes through a deep narrow chasm.

My friend John Humphries follows in the holy footsteps across Monk's Bridge.

horses have followed these routes, and some are still visible as grassy tracks while others have developed into main roads.

These old 'packhorse bridges' have very low parapets and the reason lies in the method of loading each individual horse with its cargo. Each animal had a pair of wide panniers or baskets slung across its back, one on each side, which would have made negotiating a narrow footbridge with high parapets impossible. The goods carried by horses varied as much as the

Monk's Bridge is a tricky crossing without a string of packhorses!

materials produced and traded in any particular area – wool, pottery, textiles, salt, wine and even aggregates such as coal and limestone could be carried; although this would obviously put a great strain on the animals. The average packhorse could carry 2cwt (about 100kg) of burden and could cover about 20 miles in a day. William Camden, referring to the trade between market towns from the mediaeval period to the onset of the Industrial Revolution, records that, 'The amount of traffic was vast for so small a population, but nearly all of it went on foot; or rather on hoof, trotter, paw, claw and paddle. In addition to loads as diverse as fish and flowers, lime and leather, bricks and barometers, cucumbers and coals, which were carried by strings of pack-animals, prodigious herds of cattle, sheep pigs, geese, turkeys and other livestock were driven along the roads.' This description of 'strings of pack-animals' perfectly portrays how a 'train' of packhorses would have looked in the landscape. Each team consisted of between 20 and 40 horses linked together.

The individual animals each carried panniers and were characteristically of a small but sturdy breed of about 14 hands high, possibly Dales ponies. A mounted driver, or jagger, was in charge of the train assisted by a couple of attendants on foot. The leading pony wore a bell around its neck which helped keep the whole group together and gave advance warning to travellers from the opposite direction – particularly important at narrow bridges.

And, of course, smugglers used pack ponies to carry their illicit loads of smuggled brandy, lace and other contraband unloaded from small boats landing secretly at small harbours. The goods would be taken quietly inland, usually in the dead of night, to be hidden in cellars and even churches.

Monk's Bridge can be found quite easily by parking on the Ennerdale to Calder Bridge Fell

Road in the small lay-by at the junction of the road to Haile, Wilton and Egremont. Follow the wooden Public Bridleway sign to Kinniside Common, keeping right all the way downhill, following the stream, crossing it as it bears right, continue downhill and Monk's Bridge is through the last gate on the left, just about 50 yards along the grassy bank of Friar Gill.

Nenthead and the Mines

The small village of Nenthead in the North Pennines is England's highest village at 1,500ft. At one time it was a major centre for lead and silver mining, and at one time had what was probably the most productive lead mine in the country.

The London Lead Company was formed by Quakers in 1704, and the directors, in common with other Quaker industrialists, recognised a moral responsibility to their workforce. They built, amongst other things, housing, a school, a reading room, public baths and a wash-house for the miners and their families. Nenthead was the first village in the UK to have electric street lighting by using the excess power generated by the mines. The foresight of the company, and its caring attitude towards its employees, brought immense prosperity to one of the most remote and inhospitable regions in the country and laid what were to be the foundations of today's social welfare system. This was the first purpose-built industrial village in England, and the first with a free lending library, built by the company in 1833. All their workers were encouraged to read and study, especially technical subjects and chemistry, which of course would help them further develop superior smelting techniques – absolutely essential if the company was to hold on to its reputation for the best-quality lead and silver

St John the Evangelist's Church was built and consecrated in 1845 on land given by the London Lead Company.

available. Furthermore, compulsory schooling was introduced for all the village children. In return for all these benefits, however, the company did expect sober diligence from the miners.

St John the Evangelist's Church was designed by the highly respected Ignatius Bonomi and John Augustus Cory, who later became the Cumberland County Architect. It was built in 1845 and consecrated on land given by the London Lead Company. The burial ground and

Nenthead was the first purpose-built industrial village in England, and the first with a free lending library, built by the company in 1833.

The public drinking fountain which was erected by the London Lead Mining Company.

Nenthead Mines visitor centre has excellent interpretive displays.

At one time Nenthead – England's highest village – had what was probably the most productive lead mine in the country.

the parson's house were also established on land presented by the London Lead Company; they built a post office in 1848, and by 1850 a public water supply had been provided for the village.

The company operated at Nenthead until 1882, when the leases were sold to the Nenthead and Tynedale Lead and Zinc Company. They increased silver production and continued smelting until the mill closed in 1896. Eventually, however, falling lead prices and cheap imports saw many families thrown out of work and many were forced to emigrate to America and Australia.

The mines were sold to the Belgian Vielle Montagne Company who modernised zinc and lead production. They brought the last ore out of the mines on the site in the early 1900s. Production at the site gradually declined over the following years, although there was a short period of time when it was considered worthwhile to re-work the spoil heaps, but the site finally closed in 1965.

The Nenthead mines site stands on 200 acres of rugged Pennine landscape at the very heart of the North Pennines Area of Outstanding Natural Beauty. It is the largest and most important single site associated with the lead-mining industry of the North Pennines. The Heritage Centre tells the story of this dramatic, rough-hewn landscape and the tough men, women and children who worked here. It is now a Scheduled Ancient Monument where history has been forged from this high, wild and remote landscape.

The Heritage Centre was officially opened on 15 July 1996 by John Craven of *Newsround* and *Countryfile* fame and occupies the former mine workshops that have been restored by the North Pennines Heritage Trust. Here visitors can study the geology and history in the Heritage Centre and explore the site aided by self-guided trails.

Many mine explorers particularly make for Nenthead because it still has hundreds of miles

joiners and engineers. Blacksmiths made and repaired tools for the partnerships, all this was also paid for from their bargain money. The miners were only paid once a year, which was a long time to wait, so the London Lead Company advanced them a monthly subsistence payment. But, at the end of the year if they had been paid more than they had earned, their loss was carried forward to be deducted from any earnings in the next period. Fortunately for the Nenthead miners, the London Lead Company would not let anybody go hungry just because of a bad bargain. It was Thomas Dodd, the chief mine agent from 1785 to 1816, who proposed to the company, who readily agreed, that the bargain struck would guarantee a regular minimum wage to allow the miner to feed, clothe and educate his family.

The mine entrance at Nenthead.

Lead miners were used to working in cold, wet, dark conditions, although they tried to bring some comfort to themselves where they could. Most lived near enough to walk to work, for what was usually an eight-hour shift, carrying their 'bait' or lunch which they would eat underground. They collected their tools and candles from the mine shop and would often change their clothing so that they had something dry to wear for the walk home. Some miners, who came from further afield, lived in Lodging Shops near to the mine. These buildings were filled with narrow bunks that

of accessible mines. Some of the most exciting in the country can be found here, with several horse whims and a vast engine shaft in Rampghill.

The London Lead Mining Company employed mine agents who, every fourth month, decided which veins would be worked next. Miners usually worked in 'partnerships' of about four to 10 men, and these were usually made up of a group of family or friends. They calculated the price they wanted to mine one of the 'lengths' of mineral ground. The agent knew the price of lead at market and the miners used their skill to estimate the amount of lead in the vein. Between them, they struck a 'bargain' for mining the ore.

These 'bargains' were for so much per fathom of ground cut or so much per bing (8 cwt) of ore produced. If a group 'struck it rich' they worked all the hours they could. If they had gambled poorly, they were in danger of not earning anything – even the cost of candles and gunpowder had to be deducted from the final price. The miners were supported by a team of

The Bouse-teams at Nenthead Mines.

one shift got into as another left for work! The shops may have been warm and dry but they were often cramped, smelly and vermin infested. Living in such close proximity to each other caused many health problems and many miners suffered from chest complaints such as 'black spit', a condition that developed from breathing in too much dust. If they were lucky they might live to be 50, but a miner's working life often ended by the time he was 45.

The mined ore or bouse was loaded into pony-drawn tubs, brought out of the mine and tipped into 'Bouseteams' – each gang of men had its own. Nearby the rock was washed in running water, enabling the young boys and women on the washing floor to pick out the pieces of silvery galena – lead ore. Large pieces of rock were broken up for further 'dressing', the process of separating the lead ore from the other minerals. This washing process was repeated many times in many forms to separate every piece of lead ore. The men, women and boys on the dressing floors had a hard life. They spent most of their time up to their armpits in deep cold water, dressing, crushing and washing the ore ready for smelting. In winter, when the water froze, it was impossible to work outside so they found other work underground or in the workshops. The eventual introduction of water-powered machinery meant that many operations that had previously been done by hand on the dressing floors and in the smelt mill were mechanised. Waterwheels were used for pumping and winding and a large waterwheel drove the bellows that provided the air blast for the ore hearths; however, the biggest waterwheel at Nenthead – almost 50ft in diameter – was the one that drove the pumps for the condenser installed as part of the smelt mill flue system.

At Nenthead there are several interesting working examples of water-wheels.

Any ore that was not readily separable was dealt with by the crushing mill and the processed material was finally stored in the 'Bingsteads' to await smelting. Smelters had a

hot and very dangerous job. They also worked in teams and were the highest-paid workers on the site. It was their job to heat and smelt the ore to extract the pure, molten lead, which they poured into moulds to form 'pigs'. In the early days these lead pigs were transported by carrier pony, and then by horse and cart, to market on Tyneside. In 1852 the railway station opened in Alston, greatly reducing the distance the lead had to be carried before it could be loaded onto railway wagons.

It was not just sufficient for the miners to produce quantity, as a close eye was kept on the quality of the ore coming out of the mine and the ratio of lead and silver it contained. The Assayer would heat small amounts of crushed ore in small hearths to test the lead – this process was known as 'fusion' – another process known as 'cupellation' was used to test the ore for silver content, these processes were eventually replaced with chemical analysis.

On top of this testing and as a condition of the mining and smelting leases, the company made a 'duty' payment to the landowner, in the case of Nenthead, the Greenwich Hospital, at

the rate one fifth of the value of the concentrated ore.

No doubt some of the North Pennine leadminers struck it rich and became wealthy but many lived brief, hard lives in poverty. Their difficult way of life is perhaps best described in the traditional, mournful song of the washerboys, believed to be written by Thomas Raine, the Bard of Teesdale and lead miner: *Four Pence a Day:*

'The ore is waiting in the tub, the snows upon the fell,
Canny folk are sleeping yet, but lead is reet to sell
Come me little washer lad come lets away,
We're bound down for slavery for fourpence a day.

It's early in the morning we rise at five o'clock,
And the little slaves come to the door to knock, knock, knock,
Come me little washer lad come lets away,
It's very hard to work for fourpence a day.

My father was a miner he worked down in the town
Twas hard work and poverty that always kept him down,
He aimed for me to go to school but brass he couldn't pay,
So I had to go to the washing rake for fourpence a day.

My mother rises out of bed with tears on her cheeks
Puts my wallet on her shoulder which has come to serve a week,
It often fills her great big heart when she unto me say
I never thought thou would have worked for fourpence a day.

Four pence a day, me lad, and very hard to work
And never a pleasant look from a gruffy looking 'Turk',
His conscience it may fall and his heart may give away
Then he'll raise our wages to nine pence a day.'

Newton Arlosh – St John's Church

Newton Arlosh, or the New Town on the Marsh, came into being when the nearby village of Skinburness was destroyed by the sea. A church

was originally built in 1303 as a chapel of ease by the monks of nearby Holm Cultram Abbey but after the Dissolution in 1544 it fell into a ruinous state and stayed like this for about 250 years.

The original building is regarded, along with Burgh-by-Sands and Great Salkeld, as among the best examples of the fortified churches erected in the border area during the 14th century. St John's incorporates a sturdy pele tower in its fabric with the emphasis of its construction firmly on defence. The walls are

St John's Church, Newton Arlosh, is regarded as among the best examples of fortified churches erected in the border area during the 14th century.

St John's incorporates a sturdy pele tower in its fabric with the emphasis of its construction firmly on defence.

The church door is so narrow a local legend has it that whoever of the couple emerges first after the wedding will be the dominant member of the partnership!

Mary's Church at Wreay, near Carlisle (1842), which Nikolaus Pevsner considered 'one of the best [...] Victorian churches'. Sara was the child of a family of pioneer industrialists, intelligent risk takers, open to new ideas. Her father was an industrial chemist and a good friend of Wordsworth's. She was one of three children, but her brother was mentally handicapped, so Sara, the older daughter, was raised as her father's heir. Like Jane Austen's Emma, she grew up self-willed, handsome, clever and rich; although she refused to marry in case it compromised her independence. Her house near Wreay burnt down some years after her death, so no private papers survive, but there is evidence for two strong relationships, one with a young man who was killed in India, the other with her sister, Katherine.

over 6ft thick, and the entrance door is only 31in wide, with access to the pele tower through a narrow doorway in the massive wall. The east window, the most important in any church, is only 11in wide and believed to be the smallest in any church. During the all-too-frequent Scottish raids, the villagers would round up their animals and take refuge with their priest until it was once more considered safe to emerge from the building. Because the church door is so narrow a local legend has it that whoever of the couple emerges first after a wedding will be the dominant force in the partnership!

In 1843, thanks to the extraordinary talent of Sarah Losh (1785–1853) the church was restored and extended. She is credited with the stone rams' heads beside the altar and with the eagle on the eastern ridge of the roof. The lectern with its base of bog oak is another of her works, together with a palm tree base intended as part of the pulpit. The oldest item in the church is the font, which probably came from Holm Cultram Abbey. Her masterpiece is St

Ninekirks or St Ninian's Church, Eamont Bridge

St Ninian's Church, or Ninekirks, as it is known locally, can be found about a mile along a track that winds its way through the fields alongside the River Eamont near Brougham. It is one of the oldest Christian sites in Cumbria and is worth seeking out both for its charming setting and its interesting history. From the outside the church is a long low simple sandstone building

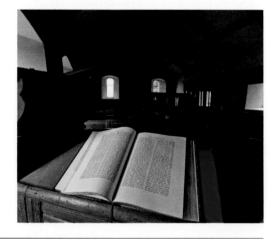

All the fittings in St Ninian's Church are of finely worked oak and display a high degree of craftsmanship.

St Ninian's Church, or Ninekirks, is built on one of the oldest Christian sites in Cumbria.

with a bellcote, protected in its natural churchyard by mature trees. Originally there was a Norman church on the site but it was rebuilt in the 1700s on the instruction of Lady Anne Clifford, who had finally inherited Brougham Castle, and who, as a devout Christian, built and restored many churches and alms houses. Her restoration work is recorded in the plasterwork above the altar, set in a wreath with her initials – AP, Anne Pembroke (the Earl of Pembroke was her second husband) – along with the date 1660. The church has remained almost unaltered since then. It is its simplicity, combined with excellent workmanship, which makes it both fascinating and memorable. The interior is whitewashed, with clear glass in the small windows and a stone-flagged floor. All the fittings are of finely worked oak and display a high degree of craftsmanship. There are box pews, family pews with canopies and an impressive three-decker pulpit. The canopied pews would have been for the exclusive use of the gentry from the castle and the nearby Hornby Hall.

Two famous warriors of long ago are buried in the church. One is Udard de Brougham, a crusader and a rebel against the Norman Kings, and the other is thought to have been a giant of a man in those days, being was well over 6ft tall, Gilbert Brougham, who fought in Normandy in the wars of King John. The church is now in the care of the Churches' Conservation Trust, which is the leading body conserving England's most beautiful and historic churches that are no longer needed for regular worship. They promote public enjoyment of these churches and encourage their use as educational and community resources.

The font dates from the 17th century.

St Ninian's Church in Brougham.

St Ninian is a shadowy, little-known figure in history. He was Scotland's first saint and it is believed that he brought Christianity to his people in AD 397. However, there is no written reference from the time when he lived and is only mentioned in works written many years after his death. According to an unbroken tradition dating from the earliest times, and confirmed in the writings of the Venerable Bede in the eighth century, a holy man named Nynia, born among the British people, introduced the Christian faith into a significant part of the land now known as Scotland long before the coming of Saint Columba.

Pendragon Castle

The present castle on the site is thought to have been built in 1160 by the Norman knight, Sir Hugh de Morville.

Pendragon Castle stands on a small knoll overlooking the River Eden and lies about four miles south of Kirby Stephen in the dale of Mallerstang. Legend connects the site with Uther Pendragon, the father of King Arthur, who allegedly tried to divert the River Eden

around his castle to create a moat, a feat commemorated by the local rhyme: *Let Uther Pendragon do what he can, Eden shall run as Eden ran.*

The present castle on the site is thought to have been built by the Norman knight Sir Hugh de Morville in 1160. He had his lands and castle confiscated in 1170 for taking part in the murder of Thomas Becket in Canterbury Cathedral. The castle became the home of the proud Clifford family and it was Robert de Clifford who extended the building by the addition of a turret on the south-west corner in about 1300. Edward Baliol, King of the Scots, was entertained in the castle when the two de Veteripont heiresses, Idonea and Isabella, lived there under the care of Roger de Clifford after their father had died of his wounds fighting for the Earl of Leicester against Henry III in 1265.

In 1341 the castle was burned by the Scots. It was later restored, only to be burned yet again by the Scots in 1541. It lay in ruins for almost 120 years until 1660 when it was repaired and made fit for habitation by the 70-year-old

widow, Lady Anne Clifford, Countess of Pembroke, Dorset and Montgomery, a great landowner and benefactor who is still highly regarded in the area of old Westmorland. She grew up in Kent and was well-known at the Court of King James I. She fought a long, hard, determined legal battle to win the right to inherit the Clifford Estates, including Pendragon Castle. She also inherited five other castles: Appleby, Brough, Brougham, Skipton and Barden Tower, which she also had repaired. She moved from one castle to another and very often stayed for a few months at a time in Pendragon. Lady Clifford took great pleasure in travelling difficult and arduous roads, shunned by others, and she would arrive over the fells in a coach pulled by six horses and accompanied by a group of servants on horseback. She died in 1676 and the castle passed to her grandson, Nicholas the 3rd Earl of Thanet, and then in 1679 it passed to the 9th Earl, Thomas, who dismantled in 1685 to save on the upkeep of several castles. Much of the material was sold off or went to repairing his other buildings.

For nearly 300 years the ravages of the weather and the plundering of dressed stone saw the castle sink into further deterioration. In 1963 the Franklands of Ravonstonedale bought the ruin for £525 and over the next 30 years the ruin was tidied up. Much of the soil and rubble hiding the walls and interior was removed, revealing hitherto unknown features such as the northern entrance to the castle with portcullis grooves and bolt holes. In 1993 English Heritage gave a grant to stabilise the exposed walls by making good and capping and re-pointing.

The castle was built from limestone and red and grey sandstone, and unusually for a Norman keep has no curtain wall. As such it is thought to be the only example of its kind in

Legend connects the site of Pendragon Castle with Uther Pendragon, the father of King Arthur.

The castle today is a romantic ruin set among the glorious scenery of the North Pennines.

The red sandstone tower of St Andrew's Church dates from the 13th and 14th centuries.

Britain. It is one of the largest in the north of England – 64 sq ft with walls almost 12ft thick – originally it had three storeys over a ground-floor basement with a great hall and a solar with vaulted chambers.

The castle remains today a romantic ruin set amid the glorious scenery of the North Pennines.

Penrith

Situated in the Eden valley to the north-east of Ullswater, Penrith is an ancient and historic market town. In the ninth and 10th centuries it was the capital of the ancient kingdom of Cumbria. The origins of the town's name are uncertain and the issue provides much material for heated discussion, but it is thought to derive from either the Celtic words *penn* and *rid* meaning 'hill ford', or *pen* and *rith* translated as 'red town'. The difficulty and indeed variation of interpretation arises because of the Cumbric language, a form of Brythonic Celtic, which was widely spoken in the area until the 11th century.

Penrith was originally built with a series of defensive gates, which allowed the population to drive their livestock into the safety of the centre of the town during the regular mounted raids by Scottish Border Reivers. Although the

gates have now disappeared, their names, such as Stricklandgate and Middlegate, remain as a reminder of former more unsettled times. Its Market Charter was granted by Henry II and it soon became an important livestock market – hiring fairs were also held here and the old market sites of Dockray, Castle Mart, Corn Mart and Market Place still form the centre of the modern town. The oldest streets, Burrowgate and Sandgate, date back to the 13th century.

The red sandstone tower of St Andrew's Church dates from the 13th and 14th centuries and is decorated with the badge of the Earl of Warwick. The rest of the church is mostly Georgian and was rebuilt in the 1720s. In the graveyard is the 'Giant's Thumb', a Norse cross dating from AD 920 and erected as a memorial to his father by Owen Caesarius, King of Cumbria from AD 920 to 937. Also in the churchyard are two 11ft-high wheel crosses combining Christian and Viking carvings. They are separated by four 10th-century hogback tombstones, and this is known as the 'Giant's

The 'Giant's Grave', the legendary burial place of Owen Caesarius, King of Cumbria from AD 920 to 937.

Far left: The 'Giant's Thumb' is a Norse cross dating from AD 920.

Left: The 1671 Robinson's School now houses the Tourist Information Centre and Museum, but was originally founded as a charity and used for educational purposes right up until 1970.

Grave', the legendary burial spot of Owen himself. The four hogback stones surrounding the grave are said to represent the wild boar he killed in nearby Inglewood Forest. Nearby is the grave of John and Mary Hutchinson, the parents of William Wordsworth's wife, Mary.

St Andrew's Churchyard was first enclosed in 1820; during the life of William Wordsworth it was described by the Reverend Eric Robertson as 'unfenced, ill kept, the scene of disorders at night and the feeding place of sheep and pigs by day'. The tudor house which dates from 1563 is

Left: The Clock Tower was erected 1861 to commemorate Sir Philip Musgrave, the second baronet of Edenhall, who distinguished himself in the Civil War on the side of King Charles I.

Far left: The tudor house from 1563 is an example of the earliest surviving domestic architecture in Penrith.

an example of the earliest surviving domestic architecture in Penrith and is widely believed to have been the home of Roger Bertram. Much later it became a school run by Dame Ann Birkett. William Wordsworth spent much of his early life in Penrith and claimed that he first attended this school when he was three. He recalls playing with the Hutchinson girls, of whom Mary was to become his wife, but it seems more likely that he and his sister Dorothy first attended the school in 1773. William boasted in later years that it only taught the upper classes of the town.

The 1671 Robinson's School now houses the Tourist Information Centre and Museum, where local history and culture and Roman artefacts are on display. The school was originally founded as a charity and used until right up until 1970 for educational pursuits.

Penrith Castle

The ruined, but impressive, red sandstone Penrith Castle was first built as a pele tower and provided protection for the townsfolk against marauding Scots. In 1397 William Strickland – later the Bishop of Carlisle – obtained permission to crenellate his tower house in 1399. He added a stone wall around the tower to further defend it against the troublesome Scots. This wall was about 5ft thick and can still be seen reasonably intact to the south-east and south-west sides of the ruins. The castle passed into the hands of the Neville family in 1419, when Ralph Neville was granted Penrith by King Henry IV. Ralph, the First Earl of Westmorland, began by replacing earlier timber buildings with stone constructions. He built the Red Tower and continued adding to the castle until it developed into a square-shaped fortress surrounding a courtyard.

When Ralph Neville died at the at the battle of Barnet in 1471, Richard, Duke of Gloucester – later to become Richard III – was granted the castle by his brother, King Edward IV. He carried on the tradition of improvements by adding the banqueting hall, a moat and additional living accommodation. He also added the north-west gatehouse. Richard himself is said to have supervised the majority of the building works

Penrith Castle was first built as a pele tower to provide protection for the townsfolk against marauding Scots.

and lodged at a local inn until they were completed. Legend has it that there was a secret passage passing from what became the Gloucester Arms Inn to the castle.

By 1565 the castle had fallen into ruin – the north-east gatehouse had collapsed and the ready dressed stone from the castle had been removed by King Henry VIII for use elsewhere. Locals also reputedly made use of the convenient supply of materials and carted off loads of stone to build their own houses and by 1572 the north-west gatehouse was in ruins and the great chamber, hall and chapel were considered beyond repair. The castle was used as headquarters by General John Lambert, the Parliamentarian, for a short time during the Civil War and even though it was already in need of repair it suffered further damage. It was further dismantled when its timber, lead and stone were sold off during the reign of King Charles I. And although it was in an even more ruinous state, the castle remained in the hands of the Crown until the mid-1690s. King William III gave Penrith Castle to the Earl of Portland in 1696, and it was later sold to the Duke of Devonshire in 1787. The duke sold the castle and surrounding grounds to the Lancaster and Carlisle Railway Company in the mid-19th century and it finally came into the possession of Penrith Urban District Council in 1914. Penrith Castle is now under the care of English Heritage.

The castle saw service as the headquarters for the Parliamentarian General John Lambert during the Civil War.

Left: After the battle of Barnet in 1471, Richard, Duke of Gloucester – later to become Richard III – was granted the castle by his brother, King Edward IV.

Legend has it that there is a secret passage from the Gloucester Arms Inn to the castle.

The Victorian viaduct carries the railway high above the Poltross Burn.

Milecastle 48 at Poltross Burn is one of the best preserved on Hadrian's Wall.

Poltross Burn Milecastle, Hadrian's Wall

Milecastle 48 at Poltross Burn is one of the best preserved on Hadrian's Wall. It was built by the Sixth Legion to a standard plan, ready to be linked into the wall as it was constructed. The milecastle measures 70ft from north to south and 60ft from east to west. The approach is by a steep climb from the burn which was probably crossed by a small bridge. The east wall has special offsets to provide a secure foundation on the steep bank. Originally the north gate was over 9ft wide but this was later narrowed to just under half the width, for improved security. The wall walk was about 15ft high and the barracks were divided into four rooms about 12 sq ft; although these were later converted to three rooms – with four rooms in each of the barracks the building could have accommodated 64 men, the maximum number possible in a milecastle. These would have been auxiliary troops – these well-trained men were not Roman citizens but were recruited from throughout the Roman Empire and, indeed, some of them would have been local. They were, however, granted Roman citizenship when they retired from the army. The milecastle was in use until the fourth century AD.

Pooley Bridge

The village of Pooley Bridge is possibly one of the earliest and most important settlements on Ullswater, and it was probably settled very early

Pooley Bridge was once a very important market town and is built around the 16th-century stone coaching bridge over the River Eamont.

The delightful old stone houses cluster around the head of Ullswater.

in the history of the area. Indeed, the Celtic tribesmen who originally made their homes here probably used their traditional method of stilt-house building in shallow water, and this almost certainly would have been one of the few parts of Ullswater in which they could have settled because in other areas the sides of the lake shoal quickly away into deep water.

The village, with its delightful old stone houses, clusters around the River Eamont at the head of the lake and is graced by its beautiful 16th-century bridge. A busy market once thrived here and fishing and farming provided most of the business, but that was before the expansion of nearby Penrith in the 19th century, although the area still has a plentiful supply of trout and salmon to attract the fishermen. Several boats are moored here and the Ullswater Steamers offer trips along the 7-mile lake to Howtown and Glenridding at its southern end. These boats are a legacy of the

Pooley Bridge has a resident paddling of very hungry ducks!

19th-century Ullswater Navigation and Transit Company steamers which provided transport for mail, goods and people around Ullswater. An excellent circular tour is to take a boat from Pooley Bridge, leave the boat at Howtown and walk to Glenridding to catch the boat back to Pooley Bridge. This was one of Wordsworth's favourites and offers fine views of the lake and Helvellyn. Not far from the village was the home of the anti-slave advocate Thomas Clarkson, whose wife was a close friend of Dorothy Wordsworth and she and William stayed many times.

The Victorian church, dedicated to St Paul, was built in 1868. The remains of an Iron Age fort can be found on the nearby Dunmallard Hill – the sinister translation is the hill of slaughter – across the bridge from the village.

Port Carlisle and the Dandy Railway

About a mile to the east of Bowness are the remains of the 19th-century harbour of Port Carlisle with its old docking quay constructed from huge sandstone blocks. The lock entrance to the 'basin' is still impressive, although this is long since silted up.

The village of Port Carlisle was originally known as Fishers Cross and developed as a port in 1819 to handle goods for Carlisle using a canal link built in 1823. It cost over £73,000 to build and William Chapman, the noted canal designer, was appointed as consulting engineer. The canal was 54ft wide with an 8ft-deep waterway and was just over 11 miles long. It had eight locks which were all built 18ft wide.

From a wooden jetty, through the sea lock entrance and through one other, the canal ran level for nearly six miles. Then there were six locks in one and a quarter miles, but it finally followed a level stretch to Carlisle Basin. It was

along this canal that boats were towed from Port Carlisle to the centre of the City of Carlisle in one hour and 40 minutes allowing Carlisle to be reached in only one day by sea from Liverpool. It allowed barges carrying the grain and produce destined for Carlisle's biscuit and feed mills right into in the canal basin behind the present Carrs (McVities) factory in the centre of the city.

Initially the venture was a commercial success because Carlisle no longer had to suffer Maryport harbour's expensive tariffs. However, the first flush of success faded and the company's poor share dividends forced it to diversify by buying boats to carry passengers on pleasure trips. However, in 1839 over 1,000 German emigrants, using what was found to be the cheapest route, sailed into Newcastle, travelled by rail to Carlisle and along the canal to board their steamer at Port Carlisle to sail to Liverpool and thence to America. An improved stone dock was opened in 1840 but severe competition from local railways made the canal unprofitable and in 1853 it was drained and its course was laid with a railway line and the first trains were running by the middle of 1854.

Passenger numbers were never very high but the line suffered further setback in 1856 when a new jetty was opened in Silloth and the Liverpool steamers began to use the deep water port there in preference to the tidal Port Carlisle. Consequentially, the train service from the city to Port Carlisle was withdrawn and replaced it with the horse-drawn 'Dandy'. Within the short space of three months the horse had saved almost 2,000 'engine miles' and by 1908 Port Carlisle had become so popular as a seaside resort that 'Dandy No. 2' was brought into service. The Dandys were very reliable and successful but in 1914 the owners of the line since 1862, the North British Railway Company, improved the track and re-introduced steam locomotives on a wave of expectation of new

The lock entrance to the 'basin' is still impressive, although this is long since silted up.

The village of Port Carlisle was originally known as Fisher's Cross and developed as a port in 1819 to handle goods for Carlisle using a canal link, built in 1823.

The remains of the 19th-century harbour of Port Carlisle with its old docking quay constructed from huge sandstone blocks.

investment for Port Carlisle. However, the outcome was that Port Carlisle could not compete with the attractions at Silloth and in 1932 the line closed for good.

It was William the First Earl of Lonsdale who rebuilt Fisher's Cross, or Port Carlisle, as it became known, with its elegant Georgian style houses between the 1800s and the 1830s. The Solway Hotel provided comfortable accommodation for steamer passengers waiting for the turn of the tide and for weekend visitors

and the Victoria Baths with its sophisticated filtering system to ensure the purest sea water for bathing provided further luxury amenities. Today Port Carlisle is a wonderful place to peacefully contemplate Victorian enterprise and grandeur.

Ravenglass Roman Bath-house

The only remaining sign of the 300-year Roman occupation of the town of Ravenglass is the well-preserved bath-house at Wall's Plantation. These impressive remains, erroneously known as Walls Castle, are among the tallest Roman structures surviving in northern England today and are located around a quarter of a mile east of the town, just off a minor road leading from the A595, past the caravan site. The bath-house was established in AD 130 and measures about 40ft by 90ft, with walls still standing at over 12ft high, which follow a zig-zag angular design suggesting the intricate structure of the original building which offered everything from hot

The only sign of the 300-year Roman occupation of the town of Ravenglass is the well-preserved bath-house at Wall's Plantation.

saunas to cold baths. Both round-topped arches can still be clearly seen and there are large areas of the internal rendering on the walls still visible. However, much of the bath-house complex, including the hypocaust flooring, which was discovered during excavations in 1881, is buried under a field to the east. Little else remains of the Roman fort of Glannoventa which was built to guard what was probably an important naval base, command centre and supply distribution point. Much of the North West was supplied from Ravenglass, serviced by a Roman road over Hardknott Pass to the Roman fort at Ambleside. Ravenglass was occupied by the Romans for over 300 years, and had a garrison of over 1,000 soldiers. Lead seals discovered during excavations here provide

evidence that the First Cohort of the Aelian Fleet was based here, a part of the Classis Britannica, or the Roman Naval British fleet.

The fort was occupied from AD 78 to well into the third century and probably marked the southern extremity of the 'Western Sea Defences', a line of forts and watch-towers erected along the north-western Cumbrian coast. The Roman name of Glannoventa derives from Celtic origins and was possibly formed from the words *glan* or *glenn* meaning 'bank, shore or landing' and *venta* translated as 'market or trading-station'.

After the Roman occupation the Norsemen and the Saxons used the port extensively. It was granted a Market Charter in 1208 by King John and indeed it enjoyed further prosperity when

The bath-house was built in AD 130 and measures about 40ft by 90ft, with walls still standing at over 12ft high, which were once mistakenly known as Walls Castle.

slate quarried in the Lake District was loaded onto boats in the harbour. Sadly, its importance as a port declined during the Industrial Revolution and other places nearer to the centres of manufacturing and industry were brought into use. The port eventually silted up through disuse; although Ravenglass has now regained its importance as an attractive coastal village rich in history, and heritage set amid beautiful scenery.

The unique Roman bath-house at Ravenglass is now in the care of English Heritage.

Ravenstonedale

Ravenstonedale is an ancient, unspoiled, picturesque village that lies peacefully at the foot of the Howgill Fells not far from Tebay, about four miles south of Kirkby Stephen. St Oswald's Church, which dates mainly from the 18th century, was erected on the site of a previous church, with a few fragments of the older building incorporated into its fabric. The approach is by a long, straight path through the large, quiet churchyard, which is surrounded by tall trees. Saxon relics have been found here and indicate that Christian worship here goes back many centuries. To the left of the porch the base of a Saxon cross can be seen and is believed to be the oldest relic of Christian worship in Ravenstonedale. Unusually for a Cumbrian church, St Oswald's follows the 'collegiate' plan, where the rows of pews face into the central aisle. In the centre of the pews on the north side, and also facing the centre is the imposing, three-level, dark oak pulpit with sounding board. The church organ was built and installed in 1891 by Harrison and Harrison of Durham at a cost of £283. It was overhauled by the

original builders in 1934 but is still as built and holds an Historic Organ Certificate.

On the north side of the church are the excavated foundations of the Gilbertine Abbey built in about AD 1200, which, it is believed, would have housed about four canons plus supporting lay staff to look after them.

Gilbert was the eldest son of Jocelyn, a Norman knight, and his low-born Anglo-Saxon wife, who had settled in the village of Sempringham in the Lincolnshire Wolds. He was born around 1083 and his mother had a vision that he would be special before his birth. It was a time that was within living memory of the Norman invasion of England and he was half-Norman, half-Saxon. He is said to have been born with some form of disability and several suggestions have been made as to what it may have been – curvature of the spine being one. Whatever it was, the household servants would not eat at the same table with him. He was unfit for military service and in his very early childhood is said to have been cared for by his mother and possibly this is why he had such an affinity for women at a time when they were not usually allowed to be educated. After studying in France, he returned home and established a local school, and in his 40th year the Bishop of Lincoln ordained him priest. When Gilbert's father died he held both the position of parish priest and squire of the family domain.

Gilbert formed a small village community of seven women, who lived in a local house under his spiritual direction and under an adaptation of the Rule of St Benedict. This was to develop into an Order, with both lay sisters and lay brothers, and several other houses were to follow, mainly in Lincolnshire and Yorkshire. In all there were 13 Gilbertine houses, four for canons, who followed the Rule of St Augustine,

St Oswald's Church dates mainly from the 18th century and was built on the site of a previous church, incorporating some fragments of the older building into its fabric.

Far left: The fragment of Saxon cross in the churchyard is believed to be the oldest relic of Christian worship in Ravenstonedale.

Left: On the north side of the church are the excavated foundations of a small Gilbertine Abbey built in about AD 1200.

Unusually for a Cumbrian church, St Oswald's follows the 'collegiate' plan, where the rows of pews face into the central aisle.

and nine double monasteries, of both men and women. The Order fell out of favour for some time because Gilbert held sympathy with Thomas Becket. In his later years, too, there was a revolt led by brothers who complained of being over-worked and under-fed. Nevertheless, the Gilbertines were well supported by Rome; Gilbert himself died in 1189, aged 105, and was canonised as early as 1202. All the Gilbertine houses were destroyed at the Reformation and never re-established, and so this brought to an end a branch of monasticism which had successfully blended the male and female religious vocations with social concern by founding several leper-hospitals and orphanages.

John Ruskin

Possibly the best way to arrive at Brantwood is by the National Trust's Steam Yacht Gondola from Coniston Pier.

John Ruskin was born in London on 8 February 1819. He was one of the greatest figures of the Victorian age, being a poet, artist, critic, social revolutionary and conservationist. Ruskin made his first visit to Keswick in 1824, when he was only five years old, and the

memorial erected at Friar's Crag after his death by the efforts of Canon Rawnsley reminds us of his famous words: 'the first thing I remember as an event in life was being taken by my nurse to the brow of Friar's Crag on Derwentwater'. That first view of Friar's Crag made a deep and everlasting impression on the five-year-old boy, and years later he described the incident as 'the creation of the world for me'. After another brief stay in Keswick in 1826, the family came for a three-week holiday in the Lakes in 1830. After a trip from Windermere to Hawkshead and Coniston, the young Ruskin wrote of his experiences in *Iteriad*, a poem of 2,310 lines – a wonderful achievement for an 11-year-old boy.

Ruskin bought Brantwood on the shore of Coniston Water, in 1871, when he was 52.

In 1869 Ruskin was appointed professor of fine art at Oxford University, where he met Hardwicke Rawnsley who was studying at Balliol College. This was to be the start of a lifelong friendship. In 1875 Ruskin introduced Rawnsley to his friend Octavia Hill, a social reformer. Rawnsley and Hill were two of the founders of the National Trust in 1896 – the origins can, in fact, be traced back to Ruskin's influence. Ruskin took up the cause of conservation with great commitment and enthusiasm and many of the issues he believed in are still campaigned for – town and country planning, green belts and smokeless zones. He also campaigned passionately for free schools and libraries.

Ruskin's affection for the Lakes was so great that in 1871, when he was 52, he bought Brantwood on the shore of Coniston Water, when he heard that W.J. Linton, the wood-engraver and revolutionary, had put it up for sale. He then carried out many improvements to the house. He added the famous turret on the south-west corner which allowed him spectacular panoramic views. He filled the house with art treasures. There were mediaeval manuscripts, Pre-Raphaelite paintings, Turner watercolours and an extensive mineral collection, all of which he had accumulated on his many travels both home and abroad. Many eminent Victorians visited Brantwood, including Charles Darwin; Holman Hunt,

In 1901, the Ruskin Museum was opened by Canon Rawnsley and remains today an important place to preserve many mementoes of a great man.

Many eminent Victorians visited Brantwood, including Charles Darwin, Holman Hunt, Kate Greenaway and Henry Holiday.

Saxon crosses, and the symbols depict important aspects of Ruskin's work and life. A year later Collingwood set up an exhibition, now the Ruskin Museum, behind the Coniston Mechanics Institute. Fittingly, in 1901, the building was opened by Canon Rawnsley and remains today an important place to preserve many mementoes of a great man.

painter of the *Scapegoat*; Kate Greenaway, one of the most popular figures in British book illustration in the latter part of the 19th century; and Henry Holiday, who spent much of his time sketching views from the hills and mountains. He wrote that 'for concentrated loveliness I know nothing that can quite compare with the lakes and mountains of Westmorland, Cumberland and Lancashire'.

In 1881 Ruskin introduced the ceremony of children dancing round a maypole with ribbons. Originally the maypole was a pagan phallic symbol representing fertility and decorated with wild flowers and garlands. The May Day Dance itself was a festival in honour of Flora (the goddess of flowers), and celebrated the rites of spring. It was Ruskin who introduced the plaiting of ribbons around the pole.

Ruskin died at Brantwood on 20 Jan 1900 from a bout of influenza, and is buried in the churchyard of St Andrew's in Coniston. His grave is marked with a large, carved cross made from green slate from the local quarry at Tilberthwaite. It was designed by W.G. Collingwood, who was an expert on Anglo-

Far right: John Ruskin's grave is marked with a large, carved cross made from green slate from the local quarry at Tilberthwaite.

Right: This painting is called: Ruskin in his study at Brantwood by William Gershom Collingwood, born 1854. He had a brilliant academic career at Oxford, where he was a pupil of John Ruskin, and he later married and settled at Gillhead, Windermere.

The Debatable Land and the Scots Dike

These days the border between England and Scotland is well-defined, but from the time of Edward I to the reign of James I of England (VI of Scotland), its line was anyone's guess. The area to the north of Carlisle and to the west of Gretna, bounded on the west by the River Sark and on the east by the Esk and Liddell, to the north by Tarras Moss and to the south by the

Esk estuary, was known as 'the Debateable Land'. This small but troublesome strip was just over 10 miles long and about four miles wide; however, its ownership was hotly disputed by England and Scotland and was consequently an irritable source of trouble to both. Neither country would admit that it was owned by the other and so neither could hold the other responsible for the actions of the people who lived there. Naturally this provided a great opportunity for the worst troublemakers in the borders and created a dangerously simmering situation, fuelling an ever-increasing round of conflict and violence. The wardens thought the best way of dealing with the area was to devastate it – making it completely unfit and impossible for anyone to live there – and even though this was done on a regular basis the resilient inhabitants returned as soon as the warden's men left. It was mostly the Armstrongs who lived in the north of the Debateable Land and the Grahams, under the leadership of the notorious Long Will Graham, who lived in the south, but numerous fugitives and 'broken men' were also attracted to the area and it rapidly became necessary to make an attempt to find a permanent solution to this ugly and ever-increasing problem.

In 1540 the English tried to solve the problem by laying claim to the whole area; but the Scots strongly disagreed and proposed that it should be divided between them.

It was decided that a strong course of action should be taken before the division was agreed and in 1551 the Wardens of both countries issued a dubious proclamation to the effect that, 'All Englishmen and Scottishmen after this proclamation is made shall be free to rob, burn, spoil, slay, murder and destroy all and every such person or persons, their bodies, buildings, goods and cattle as do remain, or shall inhabit upon any part of the said Debateable Land, without any redress to be made to the same'.

And, just to emphasise the point, the Scottish Warden, Lord Maxwell, devastated the area, burning every building to the ground. There were those who firmly believed that this would solve the problem but devastation and destruction had not worked in the past and so many still felt it was better to go ahead with the plan for division, and commissioners were appointed to carry out the task.

The Scots dike was originally about 3 or 4ft high and almost 12ft across; it would appear that the construction teams started from opposite ends and slightly lost their bearings because where they should have met in the middle the two ditches missed each other by some 20ft; although the trees now cover this miscalculation!

In 1541 the Disputed Frontier was marked by a ditch and a bank dug along an East to West line from the Sark to the Esk, and is still marked on the map as 'The Scots Dike'.

Lord Wharton and Sir Thomas Challoner represented England and Sir James Douglas of Drumlanrig and Richard Maitland of Lethington looked after Scottish interests. Predictably an agreement was not reached without an argument and it was the French ambassador, who was appointed to see fair play, who settled the question by compromise.

The new frontier was marked by a ditch and a bank dug along an East to West line from the Sark to the Esk and is still marked on the map as 'The Scots Dike'. A square stone was set up at each end with the Arms of England on one side and the Arms of Scotland on the other. The dike was originally about 3 or 4ft high and almost 12ft across; it would appear that the construction teams started from opposite ends and slightly lost their bearings because where they should have met in the middle the two ditches missed each other by some 20ft.

The decree was ratified in Jedburgh on 9 November 1540 and we are told that the Scottish High Treasurer paid £1.4s for a gold and silk cord to hang on the document.

It was hoped that the division of the Debatable Land would call a halt to border raiding but it had no immediate effect. The Liddesdale Reivers – Armstrongs and Nixons – put paid to the new hopes with a wave of enthusiastic and vigorous predatory expeditions which were to continue for the next 50 years.

What was the Sellafield Visitors' Centre is now the Sellafield Centre and is mainly used for business events. A small section is open to the public at selected times.

At least the division of the Debatable Land represented a small step forward in the co-operation between the countries after the war of 1540.

Sellafield

Sellafield (formerly known as Windscale) is a nuclear processing and former electricity generating site, about a mile to the north of the village of Seascale on the Cumbrian coast of the Irish Sea. This is the site of what was the world's first commercial nuclear power station, Calder Hall, which operated from the early 1950s until 2004, and also the Windscale Nuclear Reactor (Piles) – Britain's first attempt at a nuclear

reactor to produce plutonium for the war effort, which unfortunately suffered a major overheating and fire incident in 1957. Sellafield was previously owned and operated by British Nuclear Fuels plc (BNFL), but is now operated by Sellafield Ltd and, since 1 April 2005, has been owned by the Nuclear Decommissioning Authority.

Facilities at the site include the THORP nuclear fuel reprocessing plant and the Magnox nuclear fuel reprocessing plant. The remains of Calder Hall are now being decommissioned, together with some of the other older nuclear facilities. In 1981 the name of the site was changed back from Windscale to Sellafield, it has been suggested by some observers that it was an attempt by the United Kingdom Atomic Energy Authority to disassociate the site from recent press reports about its safety.

The Sellafield site was originally occupied by a World War Two Royal Ordnance Factory, which produced TNT. After the war, the Ministry of Supply adapted the site to produce materials for nuclear weapons, mainly plutonium – a silvery, warm-to-the-touch isotope or radioactive element which can only be produced by man because it does not occur naturally; however, it corrodes very quickly and is liable to sudden transitions.

Construction of these nuclear facilities started in 1947. The site was renamed

The storm clouds gather over Sellafield Centre.

Windscale, ostensibly to avoid confusion with the Springfields uranium processing factory near Preston. The two air-cooled, graphite-moderated Windscale reactors were the first British weapons-grade plutonium-239 production facility, built for the British nuclear weapons programme of the late 1940s and the 1950s. Windscale was also the site of the prototype British Advanced gas-cooled reactor.

When the United Kingdom Atomic Energy Authority (UKAEA) was formed in 1954, it took on the ownership of Windscale Works. The first of four Magnox reactors became operational in 1956 at Calder Hall, beside Windscale, and the name of the site was changed to Windscale and Calder Works. After the UKAEA was divided into a research division – UKAEA – and a production division – British Nuclear Fuels Ltd – in 1971, the major part of the site was transferred to BNFL. Windscale and Calder Works was renamed Sellafield as part of

About a mile north of Seascale is BNFL's Sellafield Nuclear Site.

a major reorganisation in 1981 and the rest of the site remained in the hands of the UKAEA and is still named Windscale.

Sellafield also carries out a number of reprocessing operations, separating the uranium, plutonium and fission products from spent nuclear fuel. The uranium can then either be used in the manufacture of new nuclear fuel, or in other applications where its density is an adavantage. Plutonium can be used in the manufacture of mixed oxide fuel for thermal reactors, or as fuel for fast breeder reactors, such as the Reactor at Dounreay. These processes, including the associated cooling ponds, require vast amounts of water and the licence to extract over 1.5 billion gallons a year from Wastwater – England's deepest lake – that was once held by BNFL, has now been transferred to the Nuclear Decommissioning Authority.

Shap Abbey

Just over a mile from the village of Shap, nestling in a valley of the River Lowther, lie the remains of Shap Abbey which was dedicated to St Mary Magdalene and was endowed by Thomas, son of Gospatric, a Westmorland baron. It was not a particularly large establishment and consisted of a community of an abbot and around 12 canons, but it held vast lands throughout the county of Westmorland. Shap Abbey stands in a picturesque setting with nothing nearby to interrupt the beauty of the lonely and remote site. It was built in 1199 and was the last abbey to be founded in England, and it was the last to be dissolved by Henry VIII in 1540. The abbey was founded by the Premonstratensian order, also known as the White Canons from the colour of their habits. These monks originally came from Northern France and settled near Kendal in 1190. Their devotions were about midway between the strict closed Order of the Cistercians, and the more 'community aware' benevolence of the Augustinians.

At first their method of building was very similar to the Cistercian style of austerity and simplicity and the original abbey follows this pattern. Although little more than foundation

Shap Abbey was built in 1199 and was the last to be founded in England, and it was also the last to be dissolved by Henry VIII in 1540.

The Chapter House was a formal meeting chamber where the canons gathered every day to discuss business and daily work tasks.

walls survive now, from the ground plan it is obvious that the 13th-century church was of a fairly modest construction. It was about 200ft (60.6m) long and consisted of a nave with six bays, a north aisle, two chapels in the transepts, and a plain and narrow chancel. The west tower is the most prominent feature on the site and

was the only part to be built after the rules covering the simplicity of monastic church building were changed. This massive tower still stands as a memorial to one of the great builders and reformers of the late 15th century, Richard Redman. He was the abbot of Shap for almost 50 years until his death in 1505 but, as the leading English Premonstratensian of the time, he was very highly regarded and consecutively held the posts as Bishop of St Asaph, Exeter and Ely.

Shap Abbey escaped the initial phase of the Dissolution in 1536 but in 1540 the monks finally surrendered to Henry VIII's commissioners. Demolition began almost immediately; lead was removed from the roofs, stone was taken away to be used in other buildings and all the glass was removed from the windows and melted down. The Canons accepted pensions and where possible took up positions as parish priests.

By 1545 the land was granted to Sir Thomas Wharton, a local landowner, and from him it passed to the Lowther family.

In 1948 the abbey's remains were placed into the guardianship of the state by the Lowther Estate. Shap Abbey is now cared for and maintained by English Heritage.

The abbey was founded by the Premonstratensian order, or White Canons, who originally came to Kendal from Northern France in 1190.

Skinburness was an ideal place for landing smuggled goods, particularly whisky from Scotland.

Silloth and Skinburness

Silloth takes its name from the *lathes* or barns where the monks of Holm Coulltram Abbey stored their grain. These lathes were by the sea and were known as sea-lathes and over the centuries this became Silloth. The town really came into prominence in the 19th century when the two docks were opened in 1859 and 1879.

Silloth was a very popular Victorian holiday resort, noted for its clean, invigorating air. It was thought to be especially beneficial for chest complaints and was shortlisted as suitable for the convalescence of King George V. The wide, elegant, cobbled streets and elegant front and promenade with the spectacular views over the Solway were enjoyed by Carlisle holiday makers right up until the 1950s.

Skinburness is a small hamlet a mile north of Silloth, with wonderful extensive views over the sea to Dumfries and Galloway beyond. The surrounding area has been designated a Site of Special Scientific Interest and miles of unspoilt coastline offer wonderful opportunities for walking and bird watching. This shore was an ideal place for landing smuggled goods, particularly whisky from Scotland, and it is likely that the local inn was involved in this activity and there are colourful tales of cunning locals outwitting the local customs officers and

Silloth was a popular Victorian holiday resort, noted for its invigorating air, especially beneficial for chest complaints, and was shortlisted as suitable for the convalescence of King George V.

However, the structure was fixed in its present position in 1914 and a small cabin was installed on the plinth below the tower for the keeper. The light was automated in 1930 and the front light was withdrawn from service in 1959. It was, however, rebuilt in its original style in 1997 by Associated British Ports.

The unusual East Cote Lighthouse was introduced in 1864 as a mobile structure running on a short rail track.

St Bees

enjoying their tax-free whisky around a roaring winter fire. In reality it was big business but the low level of cheating by ordinary people was often given a nod and a wink by understanding excise men. However, this gradually gave way to some ruthless sharp practice from organised gangs and in the 18th century the governments of both England and Scotland introduced harsh laws on all contraband. Tensions were further increased when the death penalty for smuggling was introduced.

Between Silloth and Skinburness is the East Cote Lighthouse. This unusual lighthouse was originally introduced in 1864 as a mobile structure running on a short rail track. It was the rearmost of two lights that marked the approach channel to the port of Silloth.

Four miles to the south of Whitehaven, situated in a deep valley, is the small village of St Bees with its long sandy beach. The rocky promontory of St Bees Head, just to the north, is the westernmost point of Cumbria and is also the start of the Coast-to-Coast walk that stretches to Robin Hood's Bay in North Yorkshire. There is evidence that the Romans were the first to establish fortifications here to guard against the Irish and the Scots. Traditionally the priory is said to have been originally founded by St Bega, who is said to have fled from Ireland sometime during the late seventh century, to escape a marriage that had been arranged by her father to a Scandinavian king. The story has it that when she landed she approached the local lord – some believe this was Lord Egremont – to ask that land be granted to build a priory; he replied that she could claim all of the land that was under snow the next day, which just happened to be Midsummer's Eve! The next day the lord regretted his cleverness because three square miles of the surrounding landscape were indeed miraculously covered with snow, and, of course, he had to keep to his word. St Bega did exist but the story of her origins along with the history of the early Christian settlement on the site are probably rooted in this fascinating legend, mysteriously shrouded in the mists of time but recounted so well by Sir Melvyn Bragg in his epic novel *Credo*. More recently the story is recreated in the millennium project – a new

Silloth really came into prominence in the 19th century when the two docks were opened in 1859 and 1879.

Traditionally the priory is said to have been originally founded by St Bega.

Far right: The nave of St Bega's Priory.

statue of St Bega depicted arriving by boat from Ireland. The names of all villagers have been written on a scroll and this, along with other objects, have been placed in a time capsule buried under the base of the statue. Talented local sculptor Colin Telfer, a miner for over 20 years, made the statue from a mixture of iron ore dust and resin – his own specialist trademark material.

Some historians believe that the nunnery **was destroyed** during one of many Danish raids **but in the early 1100s,** in the reign of Henry I, a small priory of Benedictine monks was established on the site; however, it fell into ruin

St Bega's millennium statue.

sometime between 1536 and 1541 at the Dissolution of the Monasteries by Henry VIII. The domestic buildings of the priory no longer exist but part of the red sandstone church, built in the shape of a cross, was spared and used as the parish church. The monks of St Bees are remembered in a poem by William Wordsworth:

Who with the ploughshare clove the barren moors,
And to green meadows changed the swampy shores?
Thinned the rank woods; and for the cheerful grange
Made room where wolf and boar were used to range?
Who taught, and showed by deeds, that gentler chains
Should bind the vassal to his lord's domains?
The thoughtful monks intent their God to please,
For Christ's dear sake, by human sympathies
Poured from the bosom of thy church, St. Bees!

The first college established in England to train clergy, other than Oxford or Cambridge, was established in 1817 in the choir of the priory church but closed in 1895.

Left: Mysterious stone effigies in the priory.

Experts were able to do an autopsy even though this body was about 500 years old. The cause of death was found to be collapsed lung due to a chest injury. His identity is a bit of a mystery but obviously he was quite important. Some suggest he may have been Anthony De Lucy, who is thought to have died fighting abroad in 1368 – the bodies of many knights who died in the crusades were brought home, carefully preserved, to be buried in their home church. However, his real identity may never be known but he certainly died a violent death and was considered important enough for a special burial.

Far left: The ornate red sandstone door of the priory.

During excavations of the former chancel of the priory in the early 1980s, a vault was discovered in what was the middle of the aisle, where the altar would have originally stood. It contained the skeleton of a female, and a lead coffin which, curiously, contained the mummified remains of a complete body.

The church is a peaceful and evocative place and contains several well-carved grave slabs dating from the Middle Ages. Many are

St Bees Head, just to the north of the village of St Bees, is the westernmost point of Cumbria.

*St Bega's Church –
the south aisle arch
is of the Early
English style and
this dates it to the
mid-14th century.*

decorated with ornate crosses and depict knights and men at arms, including an unusual slab with the representation of an archer. Some historians suggest that some of these grave slabs may be Templar in origin, which provides a tenuous link with the mysterious St Bee's Man.

St Bega's Church, Bassenthwaite

St Bega was the daughter of a seventh-century Irish chieftain. When she was very young, she fled from Ireland to avoid marriage to a Norse king chosen for her by her father. She resolved to devote herself to the service of God and so renouncing worldly pursuits, she 'wedded herself' to the service of Jesus Christ.

When she landed at what came to be known as St Bees Head, she had in her possession a bracelet with an image of the cross, which is recorded as having a miraculous healing property. This bracelet was kept in veneration at St Bees Priory until the 12th century.

The beautiful St Bega's Church probably dates from pre-Norman times and stands by a lively stream in the grounds of Mirehouse on the shore of Bassenthwaite Lake. Although the

church is older than any other known settlement in the parish, its origin and position are still open to speculation. It stands on the route of an ancient roadway leading from Little Crossthwaite to Bowness and it is possible that the church is built at the place where St Bega resided for some time or perhaps even where she is buried, although there is no conclusive evidence of this.

The first documented history of the church dates from the mid-12th century, but some of the building has links with earlier periods. The courses of large stones, which possibly derive

*St Bega's Church
on the shore of
Bassenthwaite
Lake.*

from a Roman building, can clearly be seen in the north and east outer walls. These and the plain chancel arch are indication of a pre-Norman style of building. The original church, which really would only have had a chancel and nave, probably dates from about AD 950. The arch between the south transept and the chancel has a slight chamfer and may date from the 12th or 13th century. The south aisle arch is of the Early English style and this dates it to the mid-14th century, this was when Sir Adam de Bassenthwaite, the last male heir of his family who died in the reign of Edward II, endowed the church with a chantry chapel. The striking octagonal font dates from about 1300 and in the south aisle, there is memorial to Sir Robert Highmore, erected in the late 14th century.

The 17th-century iron hourglass stand, displayed on the south pillar of the chancel arch, was used for timing the sermon and was significantly visible to the congregation! A Royal Coat of Arms of King George II is displayed over the south doorway – it was put there at the time of the '45 rebellion to remind people where their loyalty should lie.

Most of the exterior of the church dates from when it underwent extensive renovation in 1874.

Naturally, it is not surprising that a beautiful little church in such a romantic situation would attract many distinguished visitors and in 1794, William and Dorothy Wordsworth came to the church, which features in Wordsworth's famous work, *A Guide to the English Lakes*. In 1835 Alfred Lord Tennyson visited St Bega's, the setting of which is widely believed to have provided the inspiration for the opening of '*Morte d'Arthur*':

> Sir Bedevere carries King Arthur…
> '*…to a chapel nigh the field,*
> *A broken chancel with a broken cross,*
> *That stood on a dark strait of barren land.*
> *On one side lay the Ocean, and on the one*
> *lay a great water, and the moon was full.*'

The beautiful St Bega's Church probably dates from pre-Norman times, and is beautifully situated by a lively stream in the grounds of Mirehouse on the shore of Bassenthwaite Lake.

The Wellington Pit was sited just above the harbour and cleverly built in the shape of a castle.

Whitehaven

Whitehaven is located about three miles north of St Bee's Head on Cumbria's west coast. Its history is a mixture of its small fishing village past and its fast 17th-century growth from coal and shipping. Coal mining on a small scale probably dates back to the time of St Bee's Abbey, when the monks opened the Arrowthwaite mines. And it was they who used Whitehaven's harbour to ship stone for the building of St George's Chapel at Windsor Castle.

The Candlestick Chimney was part of a colliery engine house built in 1850.

However, it was the Lowther family who transformed the small village by opening large coal mines and building what is now known as the Old Quay in 1634 – one of the oldest remaining coal wharves in England – to ship the coal.

Sir John Lowther (1642–1705) designed the layout of Whitehaven, which was the first post-Renaissance planned town in Britain, in a grid pattern centred on St Nicholas's Church. Straight streets, stone houses with blue slate roofs and grand public buildings presented a uniform and attractive town, and many of these 17th and 18th-century buildings remain as a testament to Sir John's eye for excellent design.

By the mid-1700s, markets were held three times a week along with an annual fair which attracted buyers and sellers from all over the county. In 1814 salt-water baths were opened for beach and sea enjoyment and in 1846 the Londsale Hotel was opened by the Earl of Lonsdale and quickly established a reputation as one of the finest hotels in the north.

The Lowthers continued to invest in the town by developing several piers that allowed locally-mined coal to be shipped to Ireland. The town continued to thrive and by the mid-1700s shipbuilding was a natural development in the busy port. It was here that the world's oldest registered shipping line was founded by Daniel Brocklebank, later taken over by Cunard. He went on to build 27 ships at Whitehaven. Ropes, sails, soap and candles were among the many products manufactured in the town. Even the use of steam engines to help with drainage in the mines helped another Whitehaven industry develop, manufacturing of mining equipment and steam engines.

At one time Whitehaven's coal mines extended out far under the bed of the Solway Firth but were considered extremely dangerous because of the excessive amount of gasses and faults. The Wellington Pit was sited just above the harbour and cleverly built in the shape of a

The remains of the Duke Pit once housed a 36ft ventilation fan.

castle. However, a disaster on the site in 1910 was Cumbria's worst – 136 men were killed in an explosion and fire.

One remaining monument to the coal industry is the Candlestick Chimney ventilation shaft, which was part of a colliery engine house built in 1850. The remains of the nearby Duke Pit once housed a 36ft ventilation fan.

Whitehaven eventually became the third most important port in England, and locally-mined iron ore for the furnaces of Wales was

added to the growing exports from the harbour. There were also exotic imports which included rum, sugar and tobacco from as far away as the West Indies and the Americas.

Whitehaven was once renowned as a slave port – commemorated by the 'Beilby Slavery Goblet'. Regarded as one of the finest examples of English glass manufacture, it was made in Newcastle in 1763 and engraved with 'Success to the African Trade of Whitehaven' with a slave ship on one side and the coat of arms of George III on the other.

John Paul Jones, born in Kirkbean, near Dumfries, who was serving as an American naval officer, once tried to set fire to the shipping in Whitehaven harbour. It was rather ironic because this was where he first signed up as a seaman. His skills eventually saw him regarded in the colonies as the father of the American Navy. On the morning of 23 April 1778, his ship, the *Ranger*, slid into the harbour and he and his crew set fire to three ships. However, the town's militia were alerted and stopped him from destroying 200 other ships. This raid led to Whitehaven increasing its harbour defences to almost 100 guns. The town survived another raid in 1915 from a German submarine.

Towards the end of the 1700s Whitehaven developed problems with high tides and mining subsidence and when large iron steamships

The old pier serves as a reminder of when Whitehaven was the third most important port in England.

The walled harbour has now been created a conservation area and is busy with pleasure craft and fishing vessels.

came into use, it lost its importance as a port because it was too shallow. By the late Victorian period the decline of the coal and iron industry and the development of the port of Liverpool caused much reduced commerce and the port started to decay. However, a comprehensive revitalisation of its historic buildings, sites and harbour have seen a regeneration. Today the walled harbour, along with its piers and promenades, has been created a conservation area and is busy with pleasure craft and fishing vessels.

William Wordsworth

The name William Wordsworth is forever linked with the County of Cumbria and, in particular, The Lake District. He was born in the town of Cockermouth on 7 April 1770 and was to become the most celebrated of the Lakeland Romantic Poets.

In 1783 the Wordsworth children became orphans and William and his sister Dorothy, to whom he was particularly close, were parted – William and his two brothers spending their time at their uncle's house in Penrith while Dorothy was sent to Halifax to stay with relatives.

From 1779 William lodged with Ann Tyson at Colthouse while he attended Hawkshead

A raid by John Paul Jones in 1778 led to Whitehaven increasing its harbour defences to almost 100 guns.

Grammar School, which was founded in 1585 by Edwin Sandys, who later became Archbishop of York. In 1785 the pupils were encouraged to write a poem to celebrate the school's 200th anniversary and it was this exercise that inspired young William to 'compose verses from the impulse of my own mind'. His time spent at Hawkshead with his brother Richard was a happy one, and he remained ever grateful to his headmaster William Taylor who encouraged him to read and write poetry, and another teacher, Mr Shaw, of whom he said 'He taught me more of Latin in a fortnight than I learnt in two years at Cockermouth School'. William enjoyed the freedom at school, and indeed during holidays, to read whatever he wished – Shakespeare, Milton, Spenser and Fielding were among his favourites and one of his greatest treasures was a 'yellow, canvas covered book, an extract from the *Arabian Tales*'. He also found great physical freedom at that time and spent much time roaming the surrounding countryside on long walks, riding, fishing, flying kites and ice skating. His excursions into the countryside had a profound effect on his work and he became sensitive to the power and influence of the natural world. These feelings of love, fear and beauty in the countryside were not exclusively Wordsworth's interpretation but he was probably the first poet to express these emotions with such an intensity, moulding them more and more to express a great appreciation and deep attachment for the Lakeland countryside:

Dear native regions, I foretell,
From what I feel at this farewell,
That, wheresoe'er my steps may tend,
And wheresoe'er my course shall end,
If in that hour a single tie
Survive of local sympathy,
My souls will cast a backward view,
The longing look alone on you.

Wordsworth left Hawkshead in the summer of 1787 and during the holidays was briefly united with Dorothy in Penrith. They were joined on their long walks by Mary Hutchinson, who, much later, would become William's wife.

In October 1787 he went up to St John's College, Cambridge, but the greatly exaggerated and competitive intellectual atmosphere did not suit him at all – his education at Hawkshead had been so thorough that he was considerably advanced compared to the other first-year students and consequently he spent much of his time reading the classics and Italian poetry.

In July 1790 William and a friend from Cambridge, Robert Jones, went on a walking holiday to France and Switzerland and returned to England in October. William spent Christmas with Dorothy at their uncle's rectory in Norwich. The following January he graduated from Cambridge and left for a short spell in London.

Later in 1791 he left for France, which had been in a state of revolutionary tumult since 1789. He spent a short period in Paris before moving on to Orleans. He found his year there absolutely inspirational, and, fired with the profound belief of liberty and equality for all citizens, he planned to join the Girondist Army. While he was in Orleans he fell in love with Annette Vallon, who gave birth to their daughter Caroline in 1792. The details of the affair are shrouded in mystery and speculation and it is widely thought that William and Annette intended to marry, but the Vallon family's hostility toward him and the unsettled political climate, combined with the fact that at about that time he ran out of money, forced him to return to England alone, before the birth of his daughter.

He arrived home to an uncertain future and a sense of moral guilt and in a state of intellectual confusion. He was still fired with his enthusiasm for the Revolution and he was appalled when Robespierre came to power, the

The Wordsworths lived in Dove Cottage for several happy and contented years.

advent of the Jacobin 'Reign of Terror' and all its consequences. However, it also distressed him that Britain was at war with France and he fell into a deep depression – recounted so appropriately in his work, *The Borderers*, which he started writing in 1796; although it was not published until 1842.

In January 1795 William Wordsworth inherited £900 from Raisley Calvert, a friend who died of consumption. In the Autumn of the same year another friend offered William and Dorothy a rent-free house in Racedown in Dorset. As a result of settling in the rolling hills of the West Country they met Samuel Taylor Coleridge and his brother-in-law Robert Southey. In the years ahead the close relationship forged between William, Dorothy and Coleridge was to be a fountain of great happiness and an inspiration of creativity for all

three. Such was the importance of the friendship that William and Dorothy moved to Alfoxden to be closer to Coleridge's home. They embarked on a walking tour during which Coleridge began his work on *The Rime of the Ancient Mariner*. William made what he called 'trifling contributions' to the work, including the idea of the shooting of the albatross. Coleridge in turn encouraged William with his work and the first edition of *Lyrical Ballads* was published in 1798. After a visit to Germany, where William got the idea for his great autobiographical work *The Prelude*, William returned to England and spent a little time with the Hutchinsons.

William was determined to show Coleridge his home area and they embarked on a walking tour of the Lake District towards the end of 1799. It was during this tour that William first set his eyes on Dove Cottage in Grasmere. He wrote to Dorothy saying that Coleridge was very taken with Grasmere and that he, William, had seen a small house which was standing empty that they may take…

By the end of December 1799 William and Dorothy Wordsworth moved into Dove Cottage, and they lived here for eight years. It was during this time that some of the finest poetry in the English language was written. Dorothy had firmly established herself as her brother's secretary by then, not only copying down his poems, but also adding and deleting words or passages, under his watchful eye, of course. This was a task at which she showed consummate skill and performed admirably for many years.

Within a few months Coleridge had come to live near Keswick, nearly 13 miles away, but this distance did nothing to diminish visits to each others' houses even though they had to climb Dunmail Rise. All three were strong walkers and covered the distance easily in four and a half hours. The years at Dove Cottage were a time of great happiness – it was while living here that Dorothy describes their everyday life in her beautifully written journals, describing in minute detail their illnesses and discomforts and their joys and anticipations. Her life seems to have alternated with sessions of washing and ironing (the 'big wash' every five weeks or so!), secretarial work, reading, writing, translating, copying and baking.

In her writing Dorothy describes many incidents from which William drew inspiration for some of his most well-known poetry, and reading her journals together with his work written around the same time provides a wonderful insight and an understanding of their lives together. One such instance is the famous *Daffodils* poem – according to Dorothy's journals she was with William and he was not in fact 'wandering lonely as a cloud'*:*

I wandered lonely as a cloud
That floats on high o'er vales and hills
When all at once I saw a crowd
A host of golden daffodils;
Beside the lake, beneath the trees
Fluttering and dancing in the breeze.
Continuous as the stars that shine
And twinkle on the milky way,
They stretched in never-ending line
Along the margin of a bay:
Ten thousand saw I at a glance,
Tossing their heads in sprightly dance.

The waves beside them danced, but they
Out-did the sparkling leaves in glee;
A poet could not be but gay,
In such a jocund company!
I gazed—and gazed—but little thought
What wealth the show to me had brought:

For oft, when on my couch I lie
In vacant or in pensive mood,
They flash upon that inward eye
Which is the bliss of solitude;
And then my heart with pleasure fills,
And dances with the daffodils.

Much of William's poetry was composed outdoors while he was walking and speaking out loud. His famous statement reflects this; 'Poetry is the spontaneous overflow of powerful feelings: it takes its origin from emotion recollected in tranquillity'. Composition, however, was not easy and Dorothy often writes that he worked long and hard: 'William could not compose much – he fatigues himself with altering…William worked all morning…but in vain…William worked on *The Ruined Cottage* and made himself very ill'. His struggle to find the right words often left him absolutely exhausted. He was a man who worked hard to fulfil his ideal.

In the summer of 1802 the Wordsworths' financial fortunes took a dramatic turn for the better. The long-standing debt, owed to them by their father's employer, Lord Lonsdale, was settled leaving William and Dorothy well off. They went to France to visit Annette and Caroline, and although the details of the visit again remain a mystery, when they came back to England William married his childhood friend Mary Hutchinson. They returned to Dove Cottage and William was now blessed with two ladies to look after him.

Dorothy was an intense person and had a passionate devotion for her brother and the wedding day was a particularly difficult ordeal for her – it was so bad that she lay on the bed, weak, helpless and overcome by the thought of William marrying Mary. Unfortunately the couple did not get many wedding presents, or so it was recorded, and this was probably due to the cool attitude to the marriage adopted by some of Mary's more stern relatives.

The Wordsworths lived in Dove Cottage for several happy and contented years; Dorothy seemed to have come to terms with William's marriage as well as the difficulty of them all living together in such a small cottage. In spite of what seemed an idyllic existence they were very concerned about Coleridge, whose health was failing, and tragedy struck when William's brother was drowned in a shipwreck off the treacherous Portland Bill. Happier times followed with a tour of Scotland and a visit to see Sir Walter Scott – this inspired a number of new poems and saw William complete early version of *The Prelude* in 1805.

Lyrical Ballads had been reprinted in second, third and fouth editions and in 1827 William published his *Poems in Two Volumes*, containing all his work since *Lyrical Ballads*.

Unfortunately, this work had a mixed reception – many of the review writers ridiculed his interest in subjects that they considered not worthy of the attention of serious writers – a young Byron called the poems 'Trash', and added insult to injury by dismissing them as

'Namby pamby'. Even Southey poured scorn on Wordsworth writing about 'pile-worts and daffodowndillies'. William publicly presented an air of indifference to such severe criticism but it must have upset him greatly, but it would not be the first time that a literary master had to suffer his work being misunderstood by critics who failed to understand a new and innovative approach away from the generally accepted and conventional works of the time. However, he was firmly convinced that his work would outlive the criticisms of the reviewers and, indeed, time has proved that he was right. Wordsworth's work was on the crest of a new wave of excitement of interpretation and creativity that painters and writers were embracing with great enthusiasm and which would carry them into the new age.

In spite of the great anticipation of a new artistic step the harsh realities of everyday life had to be confronted and two of William and Mary's children died when they were very young.

John, Thomas and Dora had been born by 1808 and by 1810 Catherine and William had been born and in 1811, to enjoy more space, the family moved to Grasmere parsonage. Tragically, within six months of each other the two youngest children died, and to escape the awful, haunting memory the Wordsworths moved again, to Rydal Mount. It was while living here that William was made Distributor of Stamps, a position with a salary of £300 a year, which further improved his standard of living.

The two youngest Wordworth children died within six months of each other, and to escape the awful memory the Wordsworths moved to Rydal Mount.

As he became better off his political views modified and he was no longer the radical thinker of his youth – he became much more opinionated in his Tory beliefs.

In 1820 he published the *Duddon Sonnet Sequence* and his *Guide Through the District of Lakes* in one volume – it was well received and soon the guide was published separately. It remains today one of the best introductions to the region. In 1835 he wrote *Upon the Death of James Hogg*, which possibly ranks as one of his best works. He enjoyed his increasing fame and he was always in great demand by the gentry on his visits to London. In 1842 he was granted a Civil List pension of £300 a year by Robert Peel. Robert Southey, who had been appointed Poet Laureate in 1813, died in Keswick in 1843 and William Wordsworth was offered the position. At first he refused because he thought he was too old for the job at 73, but Peel persuaded him to accept. He remains today the only Poet Laureate who did not write any Royal Poetry –

The Wordsworth memorial, Cockermouth.

WILLIAM WORDSWORTH 1770 – 1850

he said he would only write when a royal event inspired him – unfortunately none did. However, he did attend Queen Victoria's Ball, this man of 'plain living and high thinking'.

After his daughter Dora died in 1847, William went down to the field he had bought with the intention of building a house – between Rydal Mount and the main road – and together with Mary and Dorothy planted hundreds of daffodils as a memorial to Dora.

William and Mary share a simple gravestone in Grasmere Churchyard, visited by thousands of people from all over the world.

The death of his daughter, Dora, in 1848 distressed him greatly and Dorothy's decline into mental illness in her later life was also a source of great sorrow, even though she outlived him by five years.

In the spring of 1850 the 80-year-old William caught cold on a country walk, complications developed and he died on St George's Day. His wife, Mary, survived him by nine years They share a simple gravestone in Grasmere Churchyard, which is visited by thousands of people from all over the world.

At Willowford is a fine stretch of Hadrian's Wall about half a mile long which culminates at the remains of the Roman Bridge.

Willowford Bridge Hadrian's Wall

At Willowford on the edge of the village of Gilsland is a fine stretch of Hadrian's Wall. It is about half a mile in length, incorporates the remains of two towers and culminates in the impressive remains of a Roman Bridge which

once spanned the River Irthing at this point. The only surviving pier is over 30ft long and 7ft wide but excavation has shown that there were in fact three successive bridges on the site. The river has changed its course since Roman times and the bridge is now entirely on the east bank. The first bridge was constructed from stone during the reign of the Emperor Hadrian, the second bridge is thought to have had a timber superstructure and the third was an enlarged version believed to have been extended to carry the Military Way over the river. Further difficulty in the interpretation of the site is that the original turret guarding the bridge was replaced in the second construction by a larger version.

In Roman times this must have been a very impressive, and indeed busy, part of the wall, a magnificent stone bridge dominated by the nearby fort of Camboglanna (Birdoswald) with its large garrison of cavalry and later an infantry garrison from Eastern Europe.

Between each mile castle on the wall there were two turrets, which served as look-out posts or places where patrols could safely change over.

The Jane Pit, Workington

Workington is an ancient market and industrial town which is situated at the mouth of the River Derwent. Some parts of the town north of the river date back to Roman times but it was in the 18th century, with the exploitation of the local iron ore and coal pits, that Workington expanded to become a major industrial town and port.

Iron and steel manufacture have always been part of Workington's heritage, and it was here that the famous Henry Bessemer first introduced his revolutionary steel-making process with his world-renowned Bessemer Converter. On 6 November 1856 the Workington Haematite Iron Company Ltd was established to manufacture pig iron from locally mined haematite ore. Two blast furnaces were constructed at Oldside, just north of the town, and Bessemer steelmaking started in June 1877. Recent years have seen the decline of the steel industry and coal mining and the town has diversified into other forms of industry.

A great reminder of Workington's industrial heritage is the remains of the Jane Pit, which can be seen at the junction of Annie Pit Lane and Mossbay Road. It was a 19th-century coal mine which was built by Henry Curwen, lord of the manor in Workington. The site is a scheduled ancient monument and has the best surviving example of an ornate castellated style of colliery architecture that was a feature of the large landowner involvement in the Cumbrian coal industry during the 19th century.

The monument still has a gin circle and a later steam engine house and is a rare example of a coal mine that demonstrates the evolution from horse-powered winding to that of steam power. The horse gin which provided an early means of raising coal up the shaft survives as a circular earthwork immediately to the south of the winding engine house. It originally would have had a stone-lined interior and was where a gin arm or pole powered by two horses that

A reminder of Workington's industrial heritage is the remains of the Jane Pit, which can be seen at the junction of Annie Pit Lane and Mossbay Road.

Workington harbour.

rotated a winding drum to raise coal up the shaft would be sited. This method of winding was replaced in 1843 when the owner, Henry Curwen, built the engine house to accommodate a steam-powered beam winding engine.

Jane Pit operated until the mid-1870s. The mine closed in 1875 when pumping was discontinued after the sea broke into the mine, entombing 100 miners.

The pit is perhaps best remembered in the drawing by L.S. Lowry, who often stayed in Cleator Moor in the 1950s with his friend Geoffrey Bennett, who was the manager of the local National Westminster Bank.

Wreay – St Mary's Church

St Mary's Church in the attractive village of Wreay is a highly original and unusual work of architecture – it is the product of the wonderful extrovert talent of Miss Sarah Losh, who designed and built the church between 1840 and

1842 as a memorial to her beloved sister Catherine and her parents. The church is built in the shape of a Roman basilica – a rectangular building with an apse. The apse is lined with 14 pillars, and the spaces between form 13 seats. Above them are the emblems of the 12 apostles, with Christ in the centre. The church is full of symbolic carvings – fossil forms, Oriental symbols, animals, dragons, birds, insects, flowers and a selection of weird and wonderful monsters. It is a highly original work and even Nikolaus Pevsner dares to suggest it is one of Cumbria's finest pieces of Victorian architecture – he calls it a 'crazy building' but at the same time 'most impressive and amazingly forward pointing'. Praise indeed and a reflection of the effervescent imagination of its singular architect.

Sara's father, John Losh, came from an old Cumberland family – Arlosh. He attended school in Sedbergh before going on to Trinity College, Cambridge. He was a great friend of Wordsworth's and was a wealthy industrial chemist, founding the alkali works in Walker in Newcastle and the Walker Iron Works which

St Mary's Church in Wreay is a highly original and unusual work of architecture.

Wreay Church is built in the shape of a Roman basilica – a rectangular building with an apse.

were managed by his brother William, who was a close friend of George Stephenson.

There is evidence of two strong relationships in Sara's life, one with a young man, Major William Thane, who was unfortunately killed on the Northwest Frontier in the 1842 Afghan War, and the other was with her sister, Katherine, who was described as hearty and lively. Sadly, Katherine died young in 1835 and Sara decided to dedicate a memorial to her. Architecture was a passionate interest shared by the two girls and they had travelled to Italy together. Sara thus arrrived at the decision to build a church, beautified by symbolic representations and reminiscent of their travels. There are many Italian and French features in the church and the recurring themes of the conflict between life and death and light and darkness.

St Mary's apse is lined with 14 pillars, and the spaces between form 13 seats.

The striking interior of St Mary's Church shows the magnificent carvings that adorn the interior.

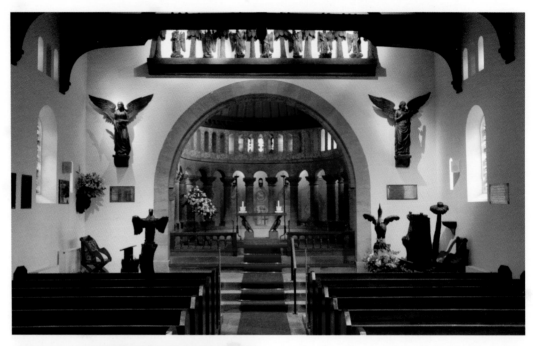

The beautifully decorated font at Wreay Church.

The church cost Sara Losh just under £1,200 of her own money – it was consecrated in 1842 and serves, not only as a monument to her parents and sister but also to an extraordinarily talented female architect, a rarity in itself, of the early 19th century. Significantly, a beautiful portrait of Sara Losh, a dark-haired, dark-eyed beauty, hangs in St Mary's Church, her masterpiece.

Far right: The beautiful portrait of Sara Losh, a dark-haired, dark-eyed beauty, is hanging in St Mary's Church, her architectural masterpiece.

The chrysalis and butterfly, a symbol of death and resurrection, is abundant as are Angels, arrows (symbolising death) and pinecones, a classical symbol of eternal life. Sara managed to persuade many of the village craftsmen to work on the church – her gardener did some of the wood carving and it is said she even sent the local mason, Mr Hindson, to Italy for a few months to sharpen his skills.

Carvings of weird and wonderful beasts decorate the exterior of the church.